UNSOLVED MYSTERIES OF THE PAST

QUEST FOR THE UNKNOWN

UNSOLVED MYSTERIES OF THE PAST

THE READER'S DIGEST ASSOCIATION, INC.
Pleasantville, New York/Montreal

Quest for the Unknown
Created, edited, and designed by DK Direct Limited

A DORLING KINDERSLEY BOOK

DK DIRECT LIMITED

Series Editor Reg Grant; **Senior Editors** Sue Leonard, Richard Williams
Editors Ellen Dupont, Nance Fyson, Deirdre Headon, Sarah Miller
Editorial Research Julie Whitaker
Editorial Secretary Pat White

Senior Art Editor Simon Webb
Designers Susie Breen, Tuong Nguyen, Mark Osborne
Picture Research Frances Vargo; **Picture Assistant** Sharon Southren

Editorial Director Jonathan Reed; **Design Director** Ed Day

Volume Consultants Maurice Geller, Lynn Picknett
Contributors Paul Begg, Peter Brookesmith, Paul Devereux, Brian Innes, Frank Smyth
Illustrators Arka Graphics, Russell Barnet, Roy Flooks, Ivan Lapper, Angela McAllister,
Richard Manning, Peter Sarson, Mark Surridge
Photographers Howard Bartrop, Mike Dunning, Martin Eidemak, Andreas Einsiedel,
Andrew Griffin, Mark Hamilton, Steve Lyne, Susanna Price, Alex Wilson

Library of Congress Cataloging in Publication Data

Unsolved mysteries of the past.
        p.   cm. — (Quest for the unknown)
"A Dorling Kindersley book."
ISBN 0-89577-359-7
1. Supernatural. 2. Parapsychology. 3. Curiosities and wonders.
4. Antiquities—Miscellanea.   I. Reader's Digest Association.
II.   Series.
BF1031.U62 1991
001.9—dc20   90-28809

Printed in the United States of America

FOREWORD

*T*HE ANCIENTS LIVE ON TODAY in the lasting monuments they left behind: the huge statues, complex sites, and massive stoneworks. The size, beauty, and primitive power of these marvels inspire a sense of wonder and awe in all of us. How the ancients, with their limited technology, could have built them is a mystery that modern science has yet to unravel. But perhaps the answer lies beyond the reach of scientific knowledge: the ancients may have been closer to hidden forces that we can no longer touch or feel. In their world with its deeper, more spiritual values, the boundaries of the unknown were thinner and more easily crossed.

Today, there are many individuals who are eager to find alternatives to science as they reassess their deepest beliefs and search for the answers to life's most enduring mysteries. Science, despite great advances, just cannot explain the many strange phenomena that continually occur around us. The unknown, which touches all of our lives, offers another, more satisfying, route to understanding the universe and our place within the greater scheme of things.

This volume explores the tantalizing challenge of the unknown, drawing in exciting new material and making surprising connections with phenomena you may already be familiar with. These bizarre and incredible events are an invitation to an increased understanding of ourselves and the mysterious forces around us. But you will need a guide to help you unlock the secrets of strange phenomena and to delve into their hidden meanings. This volume is an invaluable companion on a quest that will last a lifetime.

— *The Editors*

CONTENTS

FOREWORD
5

INTRODUCTION
THE ETERNAL QUEST
8

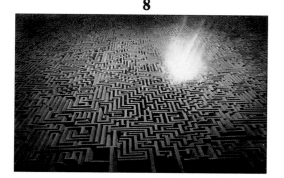

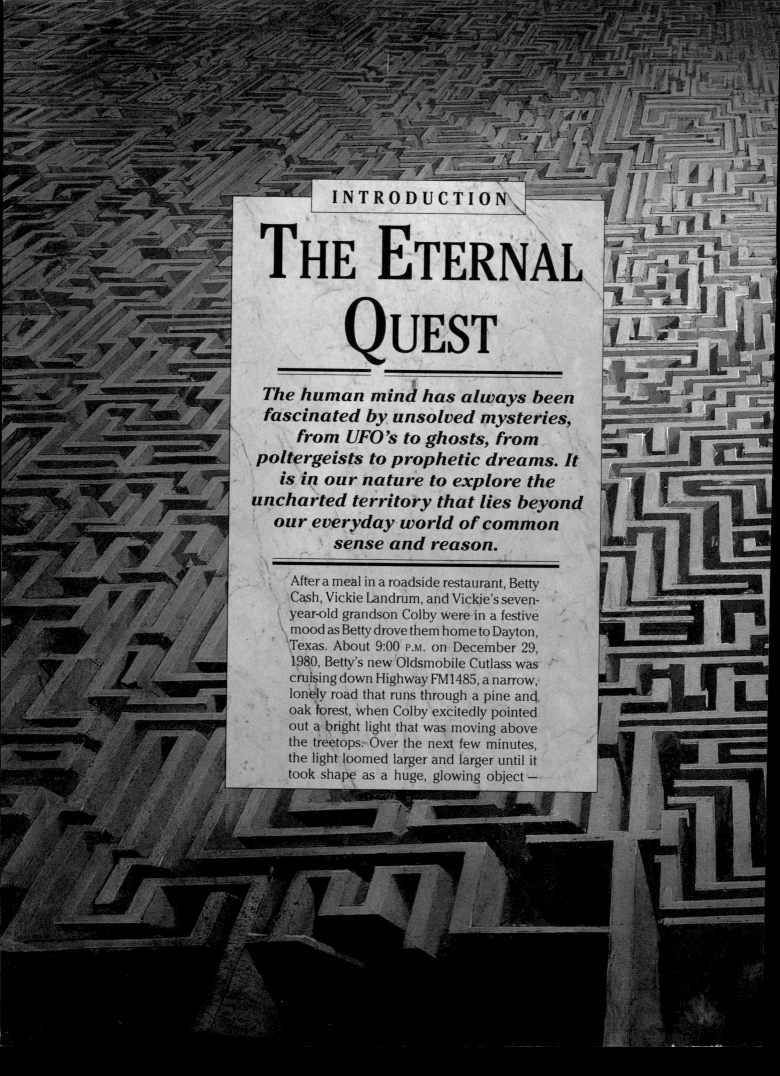

THE ETERNAL QUEST

The human mind has always been fascinated by unsolved mysteries, from UFO's to ghosts, from poltergeists to prophetic dreams. It is in our nature to explore the uncharted territory that lies beyond our everyday world of common sense and reason.

After a meal in a roadside restaurant, Betty Cash, Vickie Landrum, and Vickie's seven-year-old grandson Colby were in a festive mood as Betty drove them home to Dayton, Texas. About 9:00 P.M. on December 29, 1980, Betty's new Oldsmobile Cutlass was cruising down Highway FM1485, a narrow, lonely road that runs through a pine and oak forest, when Colby excitedly pointed out a bright light that was moving above the treetops. Over the next few minutes, the light loomed larger and larger until it took shape as a huge, glowing object —

"like a diamond of fire," as Vickie described it later — with flames bursting from beneath it. Then suddenly it was directly in their path. "Stop the car or we'll all be burned alive," screamed Vickie. Betty slammed on the brakes.

Blast of fire

The trio sat transfixed as the diamond-shaped UFO hovered above the road, just 65 yards away. From treetop level it sank to within 25 feet of the highway, emitted a blast of fire, and rose again. It did this several times, lighting up the trees and the highway all around. The occupants of the car climbed out to see the object more clearly. The UFO seemed to be made of dull aluminum, with a row of blue dots, which may have been lights, running across its center. Occasionally it made a beeping noise.

The heat from the object was terrific. Colby, frightened, begged his grand-mother to get back in the car. She did, comforting the child, but Betty remained outside. Finally the UFO moved up and away, and Betty got back in the car — which was now so hot that she could not touch the door with bare hands. Then, as the three watched from inside the car, the air was filled with the deafening noise of a swarm of helicopters. "They seemed to rush in from all directions," said Betty. "It seemed like they were trying to encircle the thing."

A giant Chinook

The occupants of the Oldsmobile drove on another five miles to a point on the highway where they could clearly see the UFO in the distance, with the flock of helicopters spread out around it. One of them, which appeared to have the distinctive shape of a giant, twin-rotor CH-47 Chinook, roared directly over

them as they watched. Altogether they counted 23 machines of various kinds around the still brilliantly shining UFO.

For Betty, Vickie, and Colby, this terrifying experience was just the beginning of the story. During the next few hours, all three developed extremely painful swellings and blisters on their skin, and suffered severe headaches and stomach pains. In just a few weeks, they all had lost some hair and had developed eye problems. Their hair eventually grew again, but to this day none of them has entirely recovered their former spirits or good health.

Did the victims share a delusion, perhaps triggered by a low-flying helicopter?

It should be said that Betty, Vickie, and Colby were not alone in seeing either the UFO or the helicopters that pursued it that night. They were simply the only ones near enough to it to be physically injured. Yet no official agency has admitted having any helicopters — let alone a fleet of 23 of them — in the area at the time. The local civil airfields and military airbases deny all knowledge of such a fleet using their facilities or showing on their radar.

Search for an explanation

So what did happen in East Texas on the evening of December 29, 1980? Was the UFO some form of alien craft that had run into trouble, and had U.S. government forces gone either to investigate or to aid it in some way? Was it a super-secret military device that had temporarily escaped the control of its helicopter escort? Does the U.S. government know far more about UFO's than it is prepared to admit? Or did the three victims share a delusion, perhaps triggered by a low-flying helicopter, which so affected them that they developed physical symptoms?

On the face of it, it seems most likely that the Texas UFO was physically real. Too many other people besides its victims saw it and its companion helicopters. Doctors said that the symptoms shown by the three victims were consistent with exposure to intense electromagnetic radiation in the ultra-violet, microwave, and X-ray bands. Vickie Landrum was convinced that a secret military device was responsible for her injuries. She and Betty Cash sued the U.S. Government for $20 million on that basis. But in 1986 the case was dismissed on the grounds that "no such object was owned, operated, or in the inventory" of the U.S. Army, Navy, Air Force, or NASA.

In a world in which such experiences as the Texas UFO sighting occur, it is not surprising that belief in the paranormal and the supernatural is so widespread.

The ancients were in touch with powers of the mind we have forgotten how to use.

There is nothing new about this: all societies in recorded history have acknowledged the existence of ghosts and spirits, and recognized the need to either harness or protect themselves against the hidden forces of the universe. The Indian tribes of North America had their shamans or medicine men; the ancient Romans consulted soothsayers and oracles; and even today the Chinese turn to geomancers, experts in *feng-shui,* for advice on the energy paths in the earth that might render a site for a building unpropitious.

In our modern scientific age, it is tempting to regard the ancient concern for the paranormal as a delusion of humanity in its infancy, and to dismiss the survival of such beliefs into the present day as a sign of persistent backwardness.

But many investigators of the unknown are prepared to turn this reasoning on its head. Writers such as John Michell, author of *A New View Over Atlantis,* assert that the ancients were in some ways superior to modern human beings — that they were in touch with powers of the mind we have forgotten how to use, and intuitively sensitive to a spiritual universe from which our materialist civilization has disastrously cut itself adrift.

Mysterious monuments

The remnants of ancient civilizations that have survived the attrition of time confront us with profound mysteries. They undoubtedly show evidence of powers well beyond anything that our stereotyped image of "primitive" peoples with only limited technology would lead us to expect.

The huge statues on Easter Island in the Pacific, the extraordinary network of lines at Nazca in Peru, the pyramids and temples of Egypt, the great stone circle of Stonehenge in England, and many other ancient sites all bear impressive witness to the knowledge and abilities of our ancestors. These ancient builders were evidently capable of precise astronomical observations and accurate mathematical computations, as well as the technical feats involved in creating these imposing monuments.

Despite the theory popularized by Erich von Däniken, that "ancient astronauts" provide the key to the great early civilizations, there is no serious reason to doubt that our predecessors created these mighty structures using their own technology and for their own ends — even if their purpose is, to us, often unfathomable.

There is plentiful evidence that, before the age of modern science, people were more at home with the paranormal. This is revealed, for example, by one of the more startling passages from that remarkable 13th-century eyewitness account of the mysteries of the East, the *Travels of Marco Polo*.

The Khan's magician

The intrepid Marco, his father and uncle, were among the first Europeans to set foot in China, arriving at Peking and the court of Kublai Khan in 1275. Among his retinue, the Khan had a number of magicians, or *bakhshi*, whose powers were considerably more spectacular than any yet shown by such modern-day wizards as Uri Geller. At court feasts, the magicians would serve the Khan in style: "When the Great Khan is seated in his high hall at his table, which is raised more than eight cubits [12 feet] above the floor, and the cups are on the floor of the hall, a good 10 paces distant from the table, and are full of wine and milk and other pleasant drinks, these *bakhshi* contrive by their enchantment and their art that the full cups rise up of their own accord from the floor and come to the Great Khan without anyone touching them."

Paranormal energy

Marco Polo makes no attempt to explain this feat; he simply swears to its truth. But the modern mind cannot be content without some attempt at a scientific explanation of such strange powers. A reasonable hypothesis is that paranormal phenomena involve an as

yet undefined form of energy that the instruments and methods of orthodox science cannot detect. But this force would certainly have to be very strange indeed, able to operate on, or perhaps through, the human mind, yet also creating physical effects such as levitation. And, unlike the forces familiar to scientists, it would need to act across time as well as space.

This "energy hypothesis" is useful, if yet to be proven, because we can apply it to all kinds of bizarre events and ask whether or not they seem to involve such a mysterious energy. In the so-called Rosenheim case, for example, it seems that only some such power could have caused the disturbances.

Pictures swung, a filing cabinet moved, drawers flew from desks, and pages ripped themselves from a calendar.

In the late 1960's a lawyer's office in Rosenheim, Bavaria, was plagued by astonishingly high telephone bills that seemed to be due to rogue equipment. Then engineers found that someone – or something – was making an astounding number of calls to the local time-of-day service. Worse, it transpired that the calls were being made faster than it was humanly possible to dial them.

Then began a series of electrical disturbances: fluorescent bulbs exploded and were twisted out of their sockets. The utility company put the office supply on to an emergency generator, but the problems continued. Pictures swung in draft-free rooms, a filing cabinet weighing 400 pounds moved of its own accord, the office photocopier repeatedly leaked chemicals although it was not switched on, the drawers flew from desks, and pages ripped themselves from a calendar.

Investigators concluded, after months of looking into every possible physical cause and coming to a dead end, that the source of all this mayhem was a young secretary who, unhappy in love and at work, was taking out her resentment on the office — albeit unconsciously. She, or the power of her mind, had caused the disturbances by bringing some force, or energy, into play that no scientific instrument could detect. When she left the company, the disturbances stopped abruptly.

The search for truth

All modern investigators into psi — a term that embraces all aspects of the paranormal from spoon-bending and levitation to poltergeists and channeling — have learned from bitter experience that they face two major tasks when investigating apparent paranormal events. The first is to establish that the witnesses were neither deceived by a hoax or practical joke, nor simply mistaken. Then, even when trickery and error have been ruled out, there remains the far more difficult issue of convincing skeptics that anything inexplicable has happened at all.

Scientific investigation

There has been serious scientific investigation of the unknown ever since the Society for Psychical Research was founded in Britain in 1882 by some of the most eminent scientists of the 19th century. Extrasensory perception (ESP), in particular, has been subjected to a whole range of laboratory tests and at one time even attracted the American and Soviet military establishments, searching for new methods of reading one another's secrets.

Experiments conducted under strict scientific conditions seem to have shown that people can learn to control

events that appear uncontrollable — for example, the score obtained by rolling dice — by the power of thought alone. This could offer an explanation for various methods of divination, such as tarot cards, I Ching, astrology, and crystal-gazing, which are all essentially attempts to foretell the future by tapping hidden forces. The order in which the tarot cards are chosen or the pattern in which the I Ching sticks fall is apparently dictated by pure chance. But perhaps they are directed by the mind of the diviner, or by an unknown force susceptible to the mind's influence — and this gives their "messages" their sometimes surprising relevance.

Tarot cards, I Ching, astrology, and crystal-gazing are all attempts to foretell the future by tapping hidden forces.

But there is also a solid body of defenders of scientific orthodoxy who have yet to concede that anything "paranormal" exists at all. Some of the classic cases of psi are, nevertheless, extremely well documented. How, for example, could the 19th-century Scottish-American medium Daniel Dunglas Home have so thoroughly boozled such large numbers of witnesses, many of them drawn from the professional and academic classes, when countless times and in good light, he poked blazing fires with his bare hands, elongated his body by 8 to 10 inches, and levitated? On one occasion, while Home was floating some 18 inches off the ground, Sir William Crookes, one of the most noted scientists of the day, passed his hands all around Home's body and failed to find any supporting device. Home never objected to such tests; indeed he welcomed them, being as bewildered as anyone as to the source of his powers.

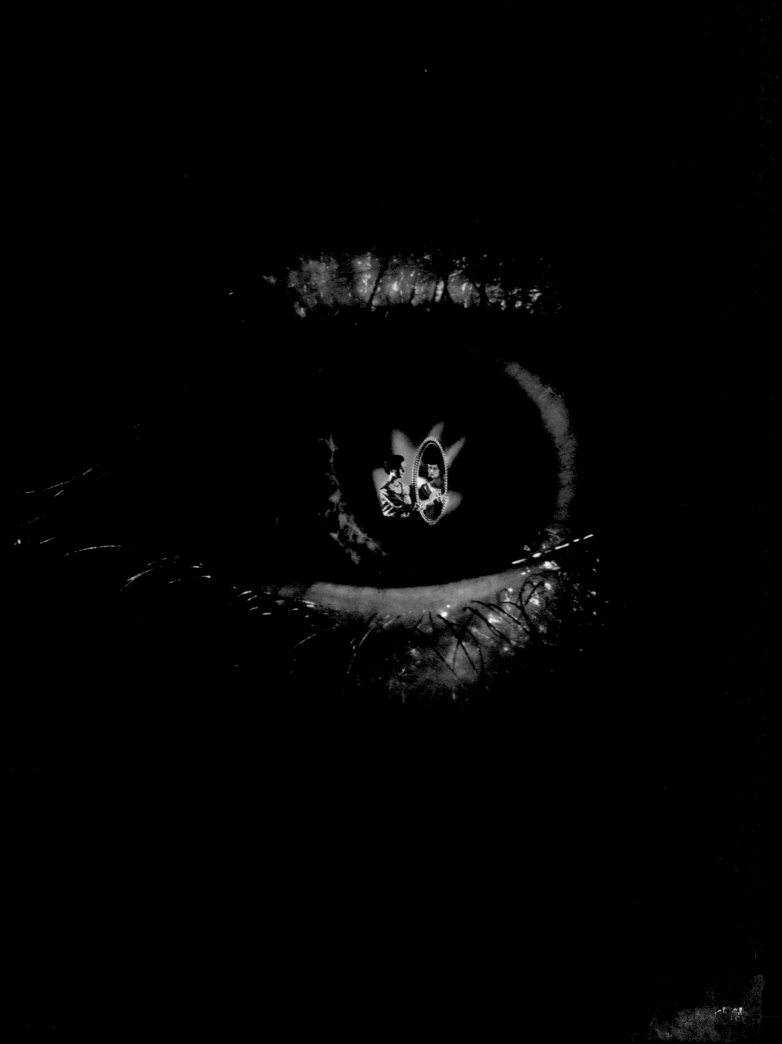

Genuine testimony, solid facts, and truly inexplicable occurrences: these are what make a real case for the existence of paranormal forces. And there is no shortage of remarkable incidents to support that case.

Mysterious appearances

Take, for example, the astonishing story of the mysterious disappearance and reappearance of the Victorian medium Mrs. Samuel Guppy. In London, England, on the night of June 3, 1871, Mrs. Guppy, who was well-known for her ability to produce fresh flowers from nowhere during séances, herself appeared out of thin air, garbed in her nightwear and clutching her accounts book and landed with a loud thud on a tabletop at a séance in a house in Lamb's Conduit Street, Clerkenwell. This unannounced arrival must have disturbed those present considerably, for Mrs. Guppy was known as "the biggest woman in London" and weighed over 230 pounds. Also disturbed, no doubt, was the friend who was sitting with her as she quietly attended to the household accounts in Highbury, some three miles away, at the moment she vanished.

Hypnotized subjects have met their previous selves in earlier incarnations.

There have also been a wealth of claims that people can move not only through space but through time, or that time itself may warp, taking people out of their own era into another.

Hypnosis has been used in recent years to "regress" subjects back into past ages, where they have supposedly been able to encounter their previous selves in earlier incarnations. The revelation that some apparent cases of regression to previous lives were definitely invalid, the supposed past lives being based on buried memories of books the subject had read in childhood, has not dampened enthusiasm for these voyages in time. Some researchers still believe they provide incontrovertible evidence for the reality of reincarnation.

Throughout history a surprising number of distinguished citizens have believed that they were not condemned to only one life on earth. Among famous believers in reincarnation have been not only writers such as Walt Whitman and Ralph Waldo Emerson, but politicians, businessmen, and military leaders, including Benjamin Franklin, Henry Ford, and Gen. George S. Patton.

Dreaming the future

Perhaps the best evidence that past and future may be strangely mixed is to be found in dreams. The number of recorded examples of "premonitory dreams" — in which the dreamer foresees some disaster and is as a consequence able to avoid it — is so impressive that hardened skeptics can only respond by blankly asserting the impossibility of the fact, whatever the evidence. One man, David Booth of Cincinnati, had a vivid dream every night for 10 consecutive nights, of a big three-engine American Airlines jet crashing. Then, on May 25, 1979, a three-engine American Airlines DC-10 crashed on takeoff at O'Hare International Airport in Chicago. David Booth's nightmares stopped. Just as astonishing was President Abraham Lincoln's dream, in which he was walking through the White House when he saw a flag-draped coffin. "Who is it?" he asked. "The President," came the reply. Just a few days later, Lincoln was assassinated. Premonitions of this kind raise the question whether, if someone can foretell the future, the future must have already happened.

FACT
The Tibetans believe that their religious leader, the Dalai Lama, is repeatedly reborn in a new human body. In 1990, Tenzin Gyatso, the 14th Dalai Lama, celebrated his 55th birthday — but if all his reincarnations are taken into account, he was actually 600 years old.

FACT
Ambrose Bierce, an American journalist who specialized as a collector of stories of mysterious disappearances, himself disappeared without trace in Chihuahua, Mexico, in December 1913.

A British medium, Matthew Manning, has even been reported to have made two-way communication across time. In the 1970's, Manning's house was haunted for a period by an entirely solid-seeming apparition who called himself Robert Webbe and claimed to be a former owner of the 17th-century house. Communicating through automatic writing, Webbe's ghost apparently informed the medium that, to him, it was Manning who was the ghost, a "ghoule of tomorrow." When Manning asked him to whom he thought he was speaking, Webbe replied: "I think sometimes I am going mad. I hear a voyce in myne head which I hear talking to me."

Backward through time

Apparent experiences of time travel have been given a new legitimacy through the amazing theories of modern physics. According to Albert Einstein's special theory of relativity (1905), time is simply another dimension. When mathematicians considering the strange behavior of subatomic particles point out that one type of particle, the positron, behaves exactly like another type, the electron, only *moving backward through time*, then anything seems possible.

Life after death

Whatever the answer to riddles of this kind, we all face one consequence of living imprisoned in a single dimension of time: our own individual death. There can be few questions in life more gripping than whether or not our personalities survive death in some form. And the history of paranormal phenomena provides a wealth of provocative but imperfect evidence that we do not cease to exist when we leave the earthly plane. In recent years, the extraordinary experiences reported by people resuscitated at the point of death have seemed to give convincing confirmation to many of the traditional religious views of life after death.

Ghostly visitations

Visions of ghosts, which might logically be taken as further reassuring evidence of survival beyond the grave, have remained a source of fear rather than hope, probably because ghosts are traditionally associated with troubled souls. This may be a genuine reflection of the "negative energy" that causes or transmits these echoes and reflections of murderers, the bereaved, or the heart-broken. But there are countless cases on record of witnesses having no sense of anything unusual or spine-chilling when encountering an apparition.

The archives of the Society for Psychical Research contain numerous reports from the First World War of young combatants appearing to a relative or friend at the moment of death.

"I saw him standing in the doorway, dressed in full flying clothes and smiling."

One such case in 1918 was related by an officer in Britain's Royal Naval Air Service, whose friend and fellow officer David McConnel had taken off in a Sopwith Camel, promising to be back "in time for tea." He came back early. His friend recalled: "I saw him standing in the doorway, dressed in full flying clothes and smiling. I remarked, 'Hello, back already?' He replied, 'Yes, I got there all right, had a good trip.' He said 'Well, cheerio!', closed the door noisily and went out." All this would have been perfectly normal, but for the fact that McConnel had died that same afternoon when his aircraft crashed at 3:20 P.M. — exactly the same time that he appeared to his friend.

While most troubled ghosts seem to be chained to the site of their unhappy, former lives, benign ghosts such as McConnel appear to be projected over long distances. Either way, these widely reported apparitions defy explanation in terms of contemporary science or common sense.

Manifestations of the unknown

A terrifying encounter with a UFO on a lonely road in East Texas seems far removed from such matters as communications with the spirits of the dead. Yet even this brief survey has shown some of the connections that may exist between different manifestations of the unknown. It is as if we were trying to investigate the nature of light, but could see it only as through a prism, broken up into its constituent colors. We would know that red light and blue light are aspects of the same thing, but would have no conception of uniting them into one clear white illumination — unless we were to take the most daring leap of the imagination.

Spirits and crystals

Imagination is certainly a quality that the New Age channelers and crystal-healers of recent years have in abundance. The explosion of New Age beliefs, especially in the United States, has centered on an optimistic faith in the untapped powers that lie concealed in the human mind.

This affirmative creed of a future irradiated with the light of the mind has reawakened interest in the whole range of unexplained phenomena. Whereas, traditionally, psychic phenomena have often been feared as a manifestation of dark forces, the New Agers in general take a uniformly positive view.

Old-fashioned mediums have been supplanted by New Age "channelers" who claim to communicate the enlightened views of spirit-beings with names like Seth and Zoosh. Faith healing has transmuted into crystal healing, exploiting the supposed vibrations of the mineral for beneficent effect. The quartz crystal, radiating clear white light, has become a symbol of cosmic harmony. Thousands of Americans have embarked on a quest to discover the secret powers of the shaman and the yogi.

> New Age beliefs center on an optimistic faith in the untapped powers of the human mind.

With visions of lost Atlantis intertwining with no less idealistic visions of a fresh future for humanity just around the corner, many New Agers seem to have abandoned the spirit of inquiry in the search for belief and reassurance.

But belief need have nothing to fear from a thorough and honest investigation of the facts — if belief is well founded. It is only through carefully considered hypotheses, tested by experiment, that the quest for the unknown can proceed on any reliable, rational basis.

Those who take up the quest know that the road will often be lonely, difficult, and lined with mocking voices. But they also know that mockery will never provide sufficient reason to renounce the challenge that the mysteries of the unknown always so tantalizingly presents.

CHAPTER ONE

ANCIENT BUILDERS

The sacred sites of vanished peoples and lost civilizations are scattered across the globe, enigmatically punctuating the landscape. Stonehenge, the Great Pyramid, the Ohio Serpent Mound, Chichén Itzá — what can these monuments of the past tell us of the wisdom of their ancient builders?

In the earliest times, when humans lived in roaming tribes of hunters and gatherers, their sacred places were natural sites, such as springs, caves, peaks, trees, or rocky outcrops, which were thought to be inhabited by a god or spirit.

But from about 9000 B.C., when people in Europe and Asia started settling down to farm the soil — the dawn of what archeologists call the

THE GODS THAT WALKED

The ancient stone statues that litter the barren, rocky landscape of Easter Island, in the South Pacific, pose an unsolved problem. They stand between 12 and 15 feet high and the largest of them weighs more than 80 tons. They were carved from rock from the dormant crater of a volcano, and we know that some were moved up to 10 miles away from the crater to their present position. But how?

Manpower

In 1956 the explorer and archeologist Thor Heyerdahl tested a theory that the great statues were moved using ropes and muscle power. Even using modern ropes, which are stronger than vine ropes, Heyerdahl's team was able to move a statue only 100 yards, not 10 miles. Even so, the head was damaged in the process. Nor could the statues have been rolled along on tree trunks, as were the stones that formed the Great Pyramid. Trees big enough to bear the weight simply cannot grow on the island's poor soil.

An Easter Island statue
Situated at Ahu Akivi, near the west coast of the island, the brooding appearance of the statue lends it an air of mystery.

Neolithic or New Stone Age — certain cultures began instead to *build* their sanctified places. On the surface of a planet previously almost unmarked by the activities of humankind, over the next 7,000 years great monuments arose. They ranged from large stones (megaliths), either erected singly or in gaunt stone circles and rows, to the sophisticated masonry of Egyptian and Mayan pyramids and classical Greek temples. Our ancestors also created earthworks, drawing vast and complex patterns of lines and images on the ground, and raising mounds to mark burial places and other sacred sites.

Awesome skills

The quantity and quality of these structures, produced with only limited technology, is astonishing. The most famous sites represent only a tiny fraction of the total of those that have survived. There are over 900 stone circles in the British Isles, for instance, and more than 800 in the West African region of Senegambia. Even in our modern age, we can only gaze in awe at the work and skill that went into the creation of a mighty megalithic monument such as Stonehenge, in southern England.

There are two questions that unavoidably come to mind when contemplating these ancient sites: how were they built, and why?

Archeologists have argued convincingly that, given the willpower and organization, ancient societies could certainly have built all these monuments unaided. But the sophistication of their design and the technical achievement

involved in their construction has provoked endless speculation that some other, more intelligent and technologically advanced civilization might have had a hand in their building.

Many of these ancient societies had myths that attributed all the wisdom and knowledge that humankind possessed to the teachings of a godlike visitor. Influenced by UFO reports and the development of

> ## On the surface of a planet previously unmarked by humankind, great monuments arose.

space travel, a new version of this idea has gained currency in recent times, suggesting that the earth was visited thousands of years ago by beings from another planet. Their powers were so great that they were looked upon as

The Ohio Serpent Mound
Built about 100 B.C., this raised mound is over 400 yards long and traces the sinuous body of a snake.

gods by our ancestors. It is claimed that it was these ancient space travelers who were responsible for the construction of some of the greater monuments.

The best known of the several writers who promoted these ideas is Erich von Däniken, with his world bestseller *Chariots of the Gods?* In his book he claimed that the enormous stone figures on Easter Island, for example, were erected by unearthly beings. Although

Wall of skulls
Lost in the heart of the Central American jungles, Chichén Itzá was the most sacred Mayan site. Of the severed heads that once decorated its palisades, only this relief now remains.

Däniken did point out some unexplained aspects of ancient artifacts and structures, many of his ideas were fanciful. Some, such as the notion of desert lines at Nazca, Peru, being landing strips for spacecraft, were demonstrably false.

Another possible explanation for the construction of the great monuments, much favored among New Age cultists, is that they were built by survivors from a former world civilization. The usual candidate is Atlantis, first described in the writings of the Greek philosopher Plato (429–348 B.C.). According to the philosopher, historians knew of a great island that lay to the west of Greece, upon which a civilization had emerged that was highly developed in technology and secret lore.

Ultimately, Atlantis was submerged by a mighty cataclysm that affected much of the Mediterranean world of its day. Only Egypt escaped destruction. Atlantean survivors have been credited not only with passing on their wisdom to the Egyptians, but also with building the megaliths of Europe and the great temples and statues of the Americas.

Borobudur
This Javanese temple dates from A.D. 800. It is intricately carved with scenes from Buddha's life.

Colossal stone giant
Hundreds of these statues are dotted over Easter Island.

Atlantis has been speculatively placed in the North Sea, the Caribbean, and the Mediterranean, as well as the Atlantic Ocean. In the end, perhaps it is best to think of the island not as a real place that might once have existed, but as a continent of the mind, a conception of a Golden Age when humankind lived in harmony with the spirits of the earth. It is just possible that the Atlantis myth may represent a dim memory of earlier cycles of civilization.

A human achievement

Many researchers find it unnecessary and even somewhat insulting to ascribe such great achievements of human genius to the influence of advanced alien beings from outer space or to the actions of strange denizens from a lost continent.

The most likely explanation of the construction of the great monuments of ancient times is simply that our ancestors were much more intelligent and skilful than our stereotypes of "primitive" societies would lead us to think. Just because ancient Egyptians did not have computers or internal-combustion engines does not mean they were necessarily incompetent or backward.

This still leaves the unanswered question of *why* these massive structures were built. Ancient civilizations certainly used many of these edifices to worship their gods, but theories about their other possible uses abound — ranging from moderately sensible and sober hypotheses to the bizarre.

The search for an answer

Some authorities suggest that the monuments are connected with ancient humanity's deep-rooted interest in the stars and the planets, that they are astronomical observatories built to calculate the seasonal movements of the sun and the moon. Other researchers, performing complex calculations based on the dimensions of these elaborate

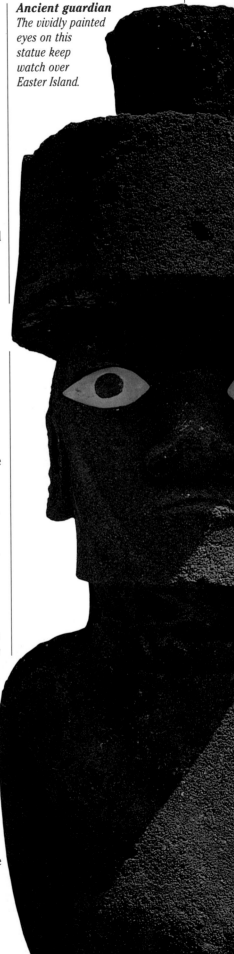

Ancient guardian
The vividly painted eyes on this statue keep watch over Easter Island.

Machupicchu
The Inca mountain fortress of Machupicchu was hidden from the world in a network of vines high in the Andes mountains of Peru until 1911, when it was rediscovered by the American explorer Stephen Bingham.

Implacable deities of stone
The massive heads of kings or gods stare at us across the centuries, a legacy of the first great civilization of Meso-America — the Olmecs. They flourished from 1200 to 500 B.C. in the fertile lowlands surrounding the Gulf of Mexico. The heads were carved from volcanic rock up to 60 miles away from the ceremonial centers where they are now to be found.

structures, have concluded that they are coded messages in stone, recording mathematical and astrological knowledge for posterity. Yet others claim that the sacred sites are powerhouses of mysterious forces, that they mark the *chakras*, or energy points, of the planet, on a global grid system only the ancient peoples were sensitive enough to perceive.

The Great Pyramid
No single building has provoked as much speculation or wild fantasy as the Great Pyramid at Giza. The term "pyramidiocy" has even been coined to refer to this outpouring of unlikely theories. Yet there is no question that the Great Pyramid truly is one of the world's

most remarkable and mysterious structures.

The largest and most important of the pyramids of Egypt, its construction was a considerable feat of engineering. Built during the reign of the pharaoh Khufu (also known as Cheops) around 2500 B.C., it is made of about 2½ million sandstone blocks, each weighing about 2½ tons. Even at 450 feet high, it is not as impressive today as when it was first built, since the top has been eroded away, and the smooth limestone slabs that once faced the steep sides have long ago been removed.

Many of the interesting features of the pyramid have led to sweeping claims about the

> **Some researchers believe the pyramids are coded messages in stone, recording knowledge for posterity.**

knowledge of the ancient Egyptians. For instance, the site of the building is said to reveal an extraordinary grasp of geography in a culture that, according to accepted history, is not even supposed to have known that the earth was round. The pyramid, it is claimed, was deliberately placed in the center of the inhabited world. This point is almost exactly on latitude 30° N and close to longitude 31° E; the two lines that cross more dry land than any others.

Of all the pyramids, the Great Pyramid is the only one to have a network of passageways built high into its structure. This has been taken to suggest that it may have been more than just a burial chamber and monument. One 19th-century astronomer, Richard Proctor, claimed that the structure had originally been built as an observatory or viewing

Pyramids at Giza
The Egyptian pyramids dominate the desert landscape.

platform, being completed as a pyramid later on. He explained the presence of the passages as being both part of the observatory apparatus and the system used to align the pyramid.

Proctor's calculations were astonishingly convoluted. He claimed that the entrance passage was aligned on the star Alpha Draconis, which, at 3° 43' away, was very close to the celestial pole (the point in the sky around which all the stars appear to revolve) in 3440 B.C. and again in

Soothsayer pyramid
This Mexican pyramid, built 2,000 years after the Great Pyramid, echoes the sacred structures of Egypt.

2160 B.C. By aligning the building around this passage, and reflecting the starlight up into a further passage above the first, the builders were able to ensure the correct orientation of the pyramid.

Microcosm of world history

Many other authorities have tried to explain why the ancient Egyptians went to so much trouble in building the pyramids. One approach holds that the dimensions of the pyramid are a mathematical code, expressing the hidden knowledge of the ancient Egyptians. The fact that the dilapidation of the structure makes it difficult to come up with exact figures for the height and length of the sides of the pyramid only fuels the fires of speculation.

Perhaps the strangest of all pyramid theories was proposed by Adam Rutherford, president of the British Institute of Pyramidology. He claimed that the layout of the Great Pyramid was a microcosm of world history, past and future, with certain points in the structure referring to specific important dates. By analyzing the pyramid he calculated that the "millennium," the final thousand years of the reign of Christ, should have begun in 1979.

PYRAMID ARITHMETIC
Did the ancient Egyptians know the dimensions of the earth? They may have, according to calculations based on the presumed measurements of the Great Pyramid when it was in its original state more than 2,000 years ago.

Multiple coincidence
A Greek writer of the second century B.C., Agatharcides, refers to the existence of a small pyramid at the apex of the main structure. This was $1/176$ the total size of the Great Pyramid. Multiplying the height of this small pyramid by the estimated total pyramid height and then by 100,000 gives a figure of 131,383,296 feet — which is the exact circumference of the earth.

The Meaning of the Megaliths

"I remember after dinner walking down to the great Carnac alignments in the moonlight...their dark shadows a reminder of their darker past and our ignorance of their makers and builders."
Glyn Daniel, *The Hungry Archeologist in France*

THE MEGALITHS, ANCIENT STANDING STONES often sited in wild and isolated locations, exert a strange fascination for modern man. They are a testament to forms of knowledge, ceremony, and ritual that are now lost in a perplexing past. Traditional archeology can tell us much about the mysterious view of the world that gave rise to these sacred monuments, but alternative approaches, perhaps less reliable but more adventurous, have also made a valuable contribution to decoding the meaning of the megaliths.

Pentre Ifan, Wales
There are thousands of megalithic monuments in western Europe. Some researchers believe these great stones were used to make observations of the sun and moon.

Stones and stars

One such approach is archeoastronomy, the study of ancient astronomies. The subject acquired a scientific basis with the work of Sir Norman Lockyer around the turn of the 20th century. A respected scientist and editor of the journal *Nature*, Lockyer established a connection between ancient buildings and the movement of the heavenly bodies. He discovered, for instance, that the axis of the Great Temple of Amon, at Karnak in Egypt, is aligned with the setting sun on Midsummer Day. What is more, on that evening, a shaft of sunlight would have penetrated to the inner sanctum at the heart of the building. Was the temple, then, built as a giant sundial, allowing the Egyptians to fix precisely the date of Midsummer Day?

Archeoastronomy came of age with the work of the Scotsman Alexander Thom in the 1960's. Inspired by the sight of the moon over the Callanish stones on the Isle of Lewis off the northwest coast of Scotland, Thom surveyed many megalithic sites. He claimed his meticulous surveys showed that many of the sites could have been used as astronomical observatories, giving readings of the movements of heavenly bodies to a level of accuracy far surpassing the needs of a simple agricultural society. For example, he asserted that the stone rows that dot the landscape of Brittany could have enabled the ancient inhabitants of that land to calculate important dates by the relative position of the moon.

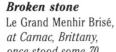

Broken stone
Le Grand Menhir Brisé, *at Carnac, Brittany, once stood some 70 feet tall.*

The shadow stone
At Castlerigg, in Cumbria, England, there is a standing stone that throws a shadow two miles long at sunset on Midsummer Day.

THE EARLY CALENDAR

Archeoastronomers claim that one of the main motives of the ancient builders was to trace the movements of the sun, moon, and stars. Their buildings were, in effect, observatories, using shadows and light beams to chart seasonal changes in the heavens. This enabled ancient peoples to measure the passage of time with great accuracy.

The first observatories

The heavenly bodies had long been used for navigation, but precise records were not possible until the construction of a fixed observatory, where the movements of the heavenly bodies could be measured in relation to unchanging landmarks. Continued observations were then gradually built up into an annual calendar, recording the seasons and the increase and decrease in the length of the day.

Callanish, Scotland

Planning ahead

Working out planting and harvest times was obviously a matter of the greatest importance to early farmers. But more than that, megalithic structures indicated the timing of the solstices and equinoxes — the climaxes of the four seasons. These dates were assigned ceremonies of thanksgiving, sacrifice, and invocation.

A MIRACLE OF SUNLIGHT

A society of Indians, living in the desert of New Mexico a thousand years ago, devised a simple but perfect instrument for measuring the passage of the seasons. And it still works today.

I N THE SOUTHEAST FACE of Fajada Butte, at the entrance to Chaco Canyon in New Mexico, stands a precise astronomical instrument. It can pinpoint the summer and winter solstices (the longest and shortest days — around June 22 and December 22), and the vernal and autumnal equinoxes (around March 21 and September 23). This miracle of engineering is built of stone, powered by sunlight, and was constructed about a thousand years ago.

Light-struck spirals

Three large stone slabs are positioned vertically against the face of the butte. The sun shines between these stones to cast daggers of light onto the rockface, and, on astronomically important days of the year, these light beams fall into key positions on two spiral carvings.

The instrument was built by a farming people known as the Anasazi, who prospered from about A.D. 800 to 1250.

Pueblo Bonito

Recently, discoveries of artifacts have suggested that the inhabitants of the Chaco Canyon were administrators of a large trading center. They constructed hundreds of miles of roads, large-scale irrigation systems, and large and complex houses, one of the most impressive of which is the 800-room, multistory Pueblo Bonito.

Given the sophistication of the Chacoan Anasazis, their creation of such a calendar is not surprising. Or perhaps the calendar came before the

sophistication, and their ability to calculate the times of sowing and planting, and the precise timing of important astronomical events, gave them the edge over all the other cultures in the region.

Whatever the truth in this chicken-and-egg debate, the discovery of such a complex system constructed from such simple components comes as a shock to the modern mind. It should also serve as an example: how much of our technology will still be functioning perfectly a thousand years from now?

Fajada Butte, New Mexico
The butte rises spectacularly out of the surrounding desert of the San Juan basin, once the home of the Anasazi people. The Anasazis created an ingenious and accurate calendar on the southeast face of the butte.

HOW THE ANASAZI CALENDAR WORKS

The sun's rays shine through the cracks between three stones to cast daggers of light on two spirals carved on the rockface behind. Four events in the astronomical year are clearly signaled. The summer solstice, when the sun is at its highest point in the sky, is marked by the dagger of sunlight exactly bisecting the main spiral at midday. The winter solstice is signaled by two daggers of light framing the main spiral at midday. The vernal and autumnal equinoxes are both indicated in the same way: the large dagger of light appears to the right of the center of the main spiral, and a smaller dagger exactly bisects the small spiral.

Summer solstice

Winter solstice

The Anasazi stone calendar

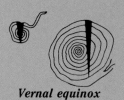

Vernal equinox

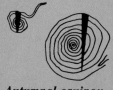

Autumnal equinox

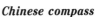

According to Thom, the stone known as *Le Grand Menhir Brisé* near the Breton village of Locmariaquer could have acted as a massive foresight for lunar observations from locations around Quiberon Bay. Now fallen and broken, its height of 70 feet would have made it the tallest standing stone in the world.

Quartz stone

It is not only temples and stone circles that have attracted the attention of the archeoastronomers. They have also studied earth mounds in Europe dating back to the Neolithic period. Some of these, which served partly as tombs, contain passageways that are almost certainly aligned astronomically. In the mound at Gavrinis in Brittany, for instance, the passage contains a single quartz stone which is placed at the

Mayan pyramid of Kukulcan
This stepped pyramid at Chichén Itzá, Mexico, casts a bizarre "serpent shadow" at the time of the vernal and autumnal equinoxes.

intersection of two separate lines, one deriving from the point where the sun rises in midwinter, the other from the most southerly point of the rising moon. Mainstream archeology has been slow to accept the validity of these prehistoric light shows. In 1989, however, Tom Ray, an astronomer at the Dublin Institute for Advanced Studies, claimed to have statistical proof that the burial chamber at Newgrange, Ireland, was deliberately arranged so that a shaft of sunlight would illuminate the tomb on Midwinter Day. The effect, Ray asserted, did not occur by mere chance.

In the United States, researchers can turn to the living traditions of the Indians for evidence of the astronomical practices of ancient man. The Hopis and other Pueblo Indians of the Southwest, for instance, traditionally practiced sun-watching as an aid to daily life. The position of the rising sun in relation to particular points on the horizon — a mountaintop or gully — told them such essential information as the time of year to sow and to harvest, and when they should observe the seasonal ceremonies required by their religious beliefs.

Looking to the heavens

Venus, the brightest object in the sky apart from the Sun and the Moon, was important to the Indian civilizations of Central and South America, particularly the Mayans, who dominated much of Central America until the arrival of the Europeans. They had learned through observation how to predict accurately the movement of Venus, as well as other heavenly bodies. This is shown by the design of the 1,000-year-old Caracol, a

---

The burial chamber at Newgrange was deliberately arranged so that a shaft of sunlight would illuminate it on Midwinter Day.

---

cylindrical tower rising from a rectangular base at Chichén Itzá, a major ceremonial center of the Mayans in the Yucatán Peninsula of what is now Mexico. The windows of this observatory align with key rising and setting points of Venus, while the diagonals of the platform on which the tower stands indicate directions of the Sun.

Also at Chichén Itzá is a stepped pyramid called the Castillo. At the two equinoxes each year, when the periods of day and night on earth are equal, the sun throws the jagged shadow of one of the stepped corners of the pyramid onto a balustrade. The shadow not only gives the impression of an undulating, slowly moving snake, but also connects with a carving of a serpent's head.

Chinese compass
The ancient Chinese put great faith in their geomancers, the experts in feng-shui who were supposedly versed in the mysteries of the earth forces. Even today, few Chinese would dare to build a house or temple without considering the balance of these occult patterns of energy. This compass was used by a geomancer in the practice of his art.

Silbury Hill, Wiltshire, England
This man-made hill is one of the most impressive of prehistoric mounds. It appears to be linked with other Neolithic sites along a straight "ley line."

The Atlantic stones

The world's most impressive megalithic sites — such as Carnac in Britanny, where this standing stone is found — form a chain spreading down the Atlantic seaboard from the north of Scotland as far south as West Africa. This has naturally led to speculation that the builders of the stone circles and rows may have migrated by sea in prehistoric times, bearing their knowledge and their customs with them.

A different approach to the meaning of the ancient sacred sites is found in the art of geomancy. The word originally described the process of telling fortunes by reading the patterns formed by casting handfuls of soil. It was given a second meaning, however, when missionaries to China witnessed the practice of *feng-shui* ("wind-water"), which the Chinese used as a method of choosing a location for houses and tombs, and deciding the way that buildings should be positioned on the site. The purpose of *feng-shui* was always the same — to balance the energies (known as *ch'i*) of the earth and the air in order to make a location more favorable for human occupancy. The missionaries used the old word "geomancy" for this system of sacred geography.

Many more geomantic systems used in other parts of the world have now been found, and researchers have learned to study sacred sites using known geomantic principles. This approach involves seeing how a site is positioned in relation to the heavens, and how it relates to its local landscape and to other sites in the region. Do the sites form alignments — usually known as ley lines?

In 1989 researcher Paul Devereux confirmed that Europe's tallest prehistoric mound,

Mystery Hill
Sunset on the winter solstice over Mystery Hill, Salem, New Hampshire. Were such megaliths actually solar observatories, used to follow the progress of the seasons?

Silbury Hill at Avebury in Wiltshire, England, combines all these aspects. Its height and position are such that the ridge of nearby Walden Hill seems to brush the distant eastern horizon when viewed from Silbury's summit. From a distinctive ledge lower down the mound, an additional skyline becomes visible,

> **One theory is that a "universal force," said to underlie all objects, is especially concentrated in the sacred places.**

which allows a "double sunrise" to be seen from Silbury at the beginning of August, the time of the harvest festival known as Lughnassadh in the Celtic calendar and Lammas in the Christian year. Moreover, Silbury forms a link in a chain of alignments between all the major Neolithic sites in the area.

Sacred centers

All geomantic schemes involve belief in an omphalos, or "world navel," the sacred center of the world from which order was created out of chaos. The holy center of Jerusalem — sacred to Judaism, Christendom, and Islam alike — is one place that has been considered the site of the omphalos. Another world navel was at Delphi in Greece. The omphalos there is a richly carved stone. The Ka'aba at Mecca in Saudi Arabia contains an omphalos fashioned from a meteorite.

The notion of ancient monuments as focal points of energy has gained popularity with researchers in recent years. One theory is that a "universal force," said to underlie all material objects, is especially concentrated in the sacred places. This force, unknown to modern science, was allegedly acknowledged in the past and sensed by worshipers at the ancient religious sites.

Most traditional peoples have, or have had, a name for some sort of mysterious life force. The Chinese *feng-shui* geomancers, as we have seen, had *ch'i*, the same energy supposedly involved in acupuncture. The Australian Aborigines have *kurunba*, which they believe is concentrated at their totem sites. In Japan the force is known as *ki*, and

Jerusalem
The Temple Mount at Jerusalem is one of the sacred centers of the earth in the old geomantic tradition.

martial arts adepts can project this force from their hands. North American Indian tribes had at least a dozen names, such as *po-wa-ha*, *manitou*, and *maxpe*, for "the force that was with them" in life.

Physical force

Questions about a universal force must remain unanswered for now. But researchers have found other intriguing energies at prehistoric sites. In the mid-1970's, for instance, dowsers and physicists confirmed magnetic effects around the Llangynidr stone near Crickhowell in Wales. Belgian researcher Pierre Méreaux found peculiar magnetic and gravity readings around the Carnac stone rows in Brittany. Sacred sites seem often to have been located close to geological fault lines, which could give rise to strange physical phenomena.

Perhaps only when we study the ancient sites from every possible angle will we begin to solve the puzzle they continue to present.

Scientific method
Since 1977, Dragon Project scientists have taken readings of radiation levels and magnetism at stone circles.

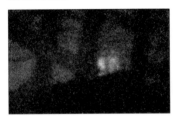

Energized stone
This Kirlian photograph of a standing stone was taken by Dragon Project researchers. Kirlian photography places an object in a high-voltage field and records the energy discharge. In the center, energy flares off the stone; in the foreground are tree shadows.

THE DRAGON PROJECT

In 1977 a Britain-based group of enthusiasts decided to subject ancient sacred sites to rigorous examination. They called their enterprise the Dragon Project, because the dragon was used in ancient China as a symbol for the hidden energy of the earth.

Radioactivity

Some sites were found to have relatively high radiation levels, mainly because of the use of granite, a naturally radioactive rock, as a building material. The King's Chamber in Egypt's Great Pyramid, for instance, is granite-clad. Some researchers believe that exposure to radiation of this kind could induce altered states of consciousness, causing visions and other "supernatural" experiences.

Magnetism

Permanently magnetic stones, capable of affecting compasses, and also weak magnetic fluctuations measurable only by sensitive instruments were found. Magnetism is also thought to alter human consciousness.

Rollright stones

Strange sounds

The tallest stone in the Rollright stone circle in Oxfordshire, England, was found to emit ultrasound (high-frequency sound inaudible to the human ear). Stranger still was the recording of babbling sounds inside an Irish stone chamber. When the tape was replayed at a slower speed, it reportedly became a voice saying: "Ghost is the listener."

Dream images

The project's most bizarre experiment is an attempt at "dream incubation." Researchers sleep at ancient sacred sites and record their dreams. The hope is that the hundreds of dreams will reveal images that are induced by the sites.

LORE OF THE STONES

Legends from many parts of the world refer to megaliths and stone circles. The tales they tell are remarkably consistent.

The Tolvan stone

HOLED STONES

Stones containing holes performed a variety of functions. The Tolvan hole at Constantine in Cornwall, England, was used in baptism ceremonies. Babies were passed through the hole nine times before being laid to sleep on a grassy knoll nearby. Similar traditions survive in connection with the Stone of Odin at Beltane in Orkney, Scotland, the Long Stone at Minchinhampton, Gloucestershire, England, and the Speckled Stone at Tobernaveen near Sligo, Ireland.

Men-an-tol stone, Cornwall

People seeking cures are passed through the ring either three or nine times in the opposite direction to the rays of the sun.

Men-an-tol stone

STANDING STONES are often attributed by folklore with the ability to move or to dance, as well as with the even more useful powers of prophecy and healing, and as bringers of good luck and fertility. For example, water splashed on the stones at the most famous stone circle of them all, Stonehenge in the south of England, was supposed to have healing properties. Another myth links the stone circle at Ka-Ur in Gambia, with that at Stanton Drew in England: the stones in both circles are supposed to be the petrified members of a wedding party.

Petrified pagan elders

The stones at Callanish in Scotland were considered to be the pagan elders of the district, turned to stone by the disapproving missionary St. Kieran. In another version of the story, a king set up the stones with the help of a retinue of priests and African workers. The priests were left behind to instruct the local people in their rituals.

This legend may have some basis in fact. The number of stone circles in the West African region of Senegambia alone is about 800, compared with about 900 in the whole of the British Isles. Africa is generally accepted as the cradle of the human race, and it has been suggested that the civilization that spawned the megaliths may have spread outwards from this continent about 5,000 years ago.

Stone circle, Kur-Batch, Gambia

Stanton Drew, Avon, England

Creative customs

Whatever their original significance, standing stones and menhirs came to be associated with fertility in the minds of local inhabitants all over the world. It was customary in many places for marriages to be consummated near the stones, and for childless women to visit the sites in a quest for fecundity.

The Iron Pillar, part of the Qutb Minar near Delhi, India, is 25 feet high and 3 feet in circumference. Local belief says that people who can stand with their back against the pillar, stretch their arms around it and then clasp their hands together, will be successful in love.

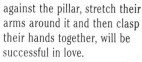

Iron Pillar, Delhi, India

Mobile megaliths

Local legend has it that the Merry Maidens in Cornwall move in the dead of night, as is the case with the column of menhirs at Menec, near Carnac, in Brittany. In Carnac 11 parallel rows of menhirs, almost 1,100 in number, and about 110 yards long, lead to a huge semicircle of stones. The myth

St. Genevieve guards her flock in this 16th-century French painting

states that the stones are petrified Roman soldiers. Every Christmas night the spell is broken and they march down to the river to drink.

Similar legends surround other ancient stones, including the Rollright stones near Oxford, England. Two large megaliths near the stone circle, the Kingstone and the Whispering Knights dolmen, are reputed to go down to a stream to drink at night. The stones themselves are said to be a king and his retinue who were turned to stone by a witch.

Merry Maidens, Cornwall

Rollright stones, Oxford, England

A saintly shepherdess

Christian missionaries often built churches on the sacred sites of the pagans, hoping to convert the local population by incorporating some of the old religion. Visions of the Madonna frequently appear at springs, while some saints are associated with stone circles. For example, St. Genevieve is sometimes depicted in a circle of stones. The town she lived in — Nanterre, outside Paris — had a stone circle that was said to be able to keep the floodwaters of the Seine at bay. The saint herself interceded with her prayers to save Paris from the ravages of Attila the Hun in A.D. 451. So perhaps this painting symbolizes the citizens of Paris (the sheep) being protected by the faith of St. Genevieve.

Fertility symbols

Stones from Scotland to Africa were shaped into phallic symbols, or carved into Mother Earth effigies. At the Christianized dolmen known as *La Pierre Chaude* in Carnac, Brittany, women would raise their skirts in front of the dolmen at full moon to invoke pregnancy. Whether the correct ritual performed at the right stone ever improved the fertility of man or woman, or even the crop-bearing potential of the land itself, has never been established.

Goddess, Oshun River, Nigeria

Phallic symbol, Ballochry, Scotland

INTERPRETING STONEHENGE

"Stonehenge is unique....Immense and still, it seems beyond man, beyond mortality. In its presence, within those silent circles, one feels the great past all around."
Gerald S. Hawkins, *Stonehenge Decoded*

Druids
Until banned from doing so in the 1980's, Druids gathered at the ancient monument to celebrate the summer solstice.

Dr. William Stukeley

FOR MANY CENTURIES, human-kind was baffled by the origins and purpose of Stonehenge, one of the world's most famous prehistoric monuments, rising dramatically out of a featureless plain in Wiltshire, England. By medieval times, legends proliferated about the ancient stones. Folk tales told of the monument's strange supernatural properties, and related how the huge bluestones were transported all the way from Ireland to Stonehenge by Merlin, the magician at the court of King Arthur. In the 18th century, the English antiquarian Dr. William Stukeley revealed to the world the fact that Stonehenge points to "the northeast, whereabouts the sun rises, when the days are longest." But this promising lead was not followed up until modern times.

Starting in the 19th century, archeologists established a number of clear facts. Stonehenge had been built over a period of some 1,200 years in three main stages. From about 3200 B.C. a circular ditch was dug with an earth bank built inside it. A ring of 56 holes, known as the Aubrey Holes, was excavated inside the bank. The Heel Stone stood outside this entrance.

Trilithons
Five of these trilithons — structures composed of two uprights and one horizontal stone — were arranged in a horseshoe formation within the sarsen circle. Three complete groups still stand. The name "trilithon" is derived from the Greek for "three stones."

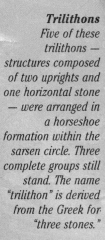

Heel Stone
This leaning stone, 20 feet high with 4 feet concealed underground, weighs an estimated 35 tons and stands within the Avenue leading to Stonehenge.

In about 2200 B.C. the Avenue was dug and the four Station Stones were installed, as was an arrangement of large bluestones. In the third stage, from

"What purpose did it serve, this monument and memorial of men?"

about 2000 B.C, the bluestones were replaced by a circle of huge sarsen (natural sandstone) boulders capped with lintels and enclosing five trilithons arranged in the shape of a horseshoe.

But as recently as the 1960's, American astronomer Gerald S. Hawkins could write: "What purpose did it serve, this monument and memorial of men whose other memorials have all but vanished from the earth?"

In fact, Gerald Hawkins, along with researchers such as Sir Norman Lockyer, Alexander Thom, Gerard Vaucouleurs, and C. A. Newham, has come closest to answering this key question. These researchers have established beyond doubt that the stones are arranged in a complex pattern related to major astronomical events. It is probable that religious rituals conducted at the sites were timed to coincide with these important occasions, regarded as sacred by our ancestors.

Sightlines
When viewed from the center of the sarsen circle, the Heel Stone aligns with the rising sun at daybreak on Midsummer Day, at the summer solstice. The existence of these sightlines was finally proved by the computer calculations of astronomer Gerald S. Hawkins in the 1960's.

The Avenue
Originally a roadway enclosed by earth banks 47 feet apart, the Avenue led to the northeast entrance along the line of the rising sun on Midsummer Day.

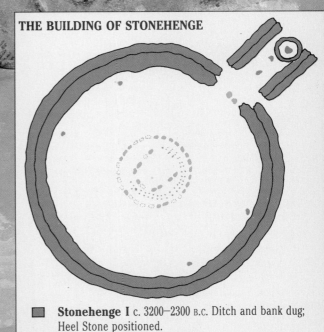

THE BUILDING OF STONEHENGE

- ◼ **Stonehenge I** c. 3200–2300 B.C. Ditch and bank dug; Heel Stone positioned.
- ◼ **Stonehenge II** c. 2200 B.C. The Avenue dug, and 2 stones set up; 4 Station Stones set up; bluestones set in horseshoe.
- ◻ **Stonehenge III** c. 2000 B.C. Trilithons and sarsen circle set up; 2 upright stones set up near entrance.

MYSTERIES OF THE MAZE

Since the dawn of civilization, mazes have fascinated humankind. Labyrinth designs appear on the stones of burial chambers in Ireland that may be 4,500 years old.

Cretan coins

A COIN OF THE SECOND CENTURY B.C., found at Knossos in Crete, has a distinctive circular maze design with seven rings. Exactly the same design appears mysteriously at different periods in history on stones and artifacts as far apart as India, Norway, Ireland, England, and the state of Arizona.

What were these mazes for? There are several theories. Since labyrinth carvings are often found near sacred burial sites, they seem to have been strongly associated with death in the mind of ancient man. They were possibly a type of magic device to ward off evil, or a symbol of the passage through life, or through the underworld after death. Or, they may simply have been an ancient sign meaning "No Entry" to the living.

Ornamental hedge mazes are a relatively recent introduction, becoming common only about 400 years ago. Those that survive in public gardens are still popular today, especially with children. It may be that the labyrinth still has a significance for our subconscious minds, while its secrets recede even further into our ancient past.

THE CRETAN LABYRINTH

The most famous maze of all is the fabled labyrinth at Knossos in Crete that housed a monster known as the Minotaur. The actual site has never been found. The legend is as follows:

Minos, king of Crete, held sway over Athens, and every nine years demanded tribute of seven youths and seven maidens. They were sent into the labyrinth (designed for the king by his brilliant engineer, Daedalus) to be killed by the Minotaur, a monster that was part man and part bull.

"Theseus and Ariadne" — Italian Renaissance painting

Theseus, a prince of Athens, volunteered to go as one of the sacrificial youths. Minos' beautiful daughter Ariadne fell in love with him, and gave him a thread to unravel on his way to the center of the labyrinth. Theseus found and killed the Minotaur, followed the thread back out of the labyrinth, and returned home in triumph to Athens.

Hollywood stone

Tintagel carving

Carved stone at Newgrange

Ancient mazes

A granite stone from the Bronze Age, about 1500 B.C., discovered near Hollywood, County Wicklow, Ireland, was found to carry exactly the same maze design as a coin minted in Knossos, Crete, over 1,300 years later. Two more Bronze Age carvings with the same design were found at Tintagel in England, and there are similar mazes in Scandinavia. They occur as a Manas-Chakra, a religious emblem, in Rajasthan, India, and as a symbol of Mother Earth among the Hopi Indians in Arizona. Even older designs based on a mazelike spiral motif appear on the entrance stone of the passage-grave at Newgrange, County Meath, Ireland, that is said to date back to 2500 B.C.

Snakes and spirals
This Australian Aboriginal bark painting, by a member of the Murinbatta tribe, is from Port Keats in the Northern Territory. Its subject is the "Great Snake," that according to Aboriginal culture is an important creative being. Labyrinthine circles and spiral designs are a common feature in Aboriginal art, and are usually associated with creative energy. The spiral is connected with birth in cultures all over the world.

Aboriginal bark painting

Ceiling maze at Mantua

A maze and a motto
The maze was adopted as an emblem by the Gonzaga family, dukes of Mantua, during the Renaissance. There is a magnificent painting of a labyrinth on a wooden ceiling of the ducal palace at Mantua, Italy. The wording around the border of the design commemorates the crusade of Vincenzo Gonzaga against the Turks. Along the path of the maze the Gonzaga family motto is repeated again and again: "Maybe yes, maybe no."

Human bone ornament
This *hei-tiki* from New Zealand is a body ornament, probably intended as a necklace. It was made in the early 19th century, from human bone. The spiral design is a traditional pattern that symbolizes the masculine principle, and is used here to signify the position of the major joints of the figure, at the shoulder and the hip.

Maori hei-tiki

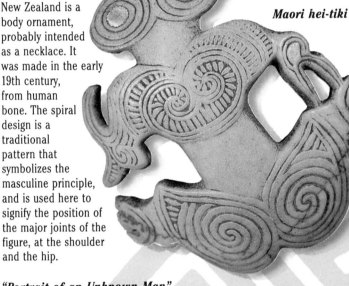

English turf mazes
Turf mazes, although not exclusive to England, are more common there than anywhere else. One of the best-preserved examples is at Wing in Rutland. Turf has been cut away from an area around 40 feet in diameter to leave a raised path that leads to the center. Its design is similar to that of the turf mazes at Alkborough in Lincolnshire and Breamore in Hampshire, and also the maze on the floor of the cathedral at Chartres in France. As with many other turf mazes, it is near the site of an ancient burial mound.

Labyrinth at Lucca

"All for love"
Painted on a wall in the cathedral at Lucca, Italy, is a labyrinth 20 inches in diameter. Probably dating from the 13th century, it originally had the figures of Theseus and the Minotaur at the center. These have long since been worn off by generation after generation of fingers tracing the complex design. A Latin inscription reads: "This is the labyrinth that the Cretan Daedalus built, out of which nobody could escape, except Theseus; nor could he have done it without the help of Ariadne and her thread, all for love."

"Portrait of an Unknown Man"

Turf maze at Wing

Mystery man
This "Portrait of an Unknown Man" is by Bartolommeo de Veneto, and was painted around 1510. The labyrinth on his chest is a symbol of secrecy. This theme is reinforced by the "Solomon's knots" on the rest of his garments, a design that combines the mystical symbols of swastika, cross, and labyrinth.

41

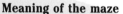

Turf maze at Alkborough

Boulder labyrinth at St. Agnes

St. Agnes stone maze

At Camperdeazil Point on St. Agnes, one of the Isles of Scilly off the southwest coast of England, there is a maze formed by a pattern of loose boulders. Boulder mazes are most often found in Scandinavia. The stone maze on St. Agnes island is called Troy Town, the name commonly given to turf mazes in England. It is likely that a ritual dance was performed there, and that the movement of the dancers through the maze in some way reflected the movement of the sun through the heavens.

A Lincolnshire labyrinth

At Alkborough, Lincolnshire, England, there is a turf maze known as Julian's Bower or Gilling Bore. It is 40 feet in diameter and the borders of the design are cut six inches deep into the turf. The design is repeated in stained glass and on the stone floor of the parish church of Alkborough, and on a tombstone in the cemetery. The first record of the maze is in a diary written between 1671 and 1704, but it is probably a lot older. A later commentator refers to "running it in and out," and to watching the villagers playing May Eve games there, "under an indefinite persuasion of something unknown and unseen cooperating with them."

Maze on tombstone

Meaning of the maze

Various theories exist as to the original purpose of turf mazes. It has been suggested that they date back to the Roman occupation of Britain and are courses for the ancient, mysterious "game of Troy." They are often found near sacred sites and probably have ritual significance, perhaps as a type of magic to ward off evil. This would help to explain how the designs became adopted by Christianity and were incorporated into some European medieval churches.

Maze in stained glass

Uppland runestone

This memorial runestone at Uppland in Sweden dates back to Viking times, about A.D. 900. It has a complex meandering design featuring serpent motifs. The lettering in the winding banner refers to the person commemorated by the stone. The snake is the Midgard, the serpent that circles the globe in Viking mythology. The serpent and the spiral are frequently seen in labyrinths.

Viking memorial stone

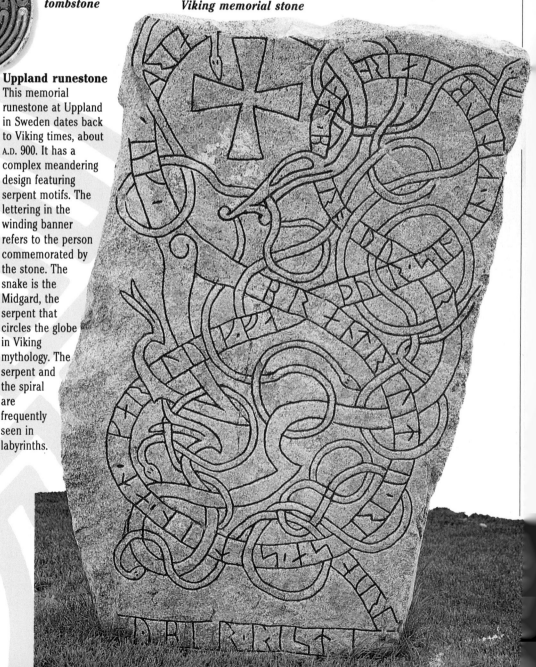

Amerindian miniature maze

This tiny basket, only three inches in diameter, was handwoven from horsehair by a member of the Pima tribe in southwest Arizona. The figure in the design is an *iitoi*, or founding father, who climbed a mountain to avoid a great flood. Having descended from the mountain to found the tribe, the *iitoi* returned to the heights by a tortuous path — symbolized by the labyrinth design.

Labyrinth design on a basket

Nazca lines

The strange lines, shapes, and mazelike spirals etched on the Nazca plains of Peru are thought to be the work of a pre-Inca civilization. Stones and pebbles were systematically removed from the ground to reveal the darker soil beneath. Some of the straight lines are aligned with stars and are reputed to have an astrological significance. The purpose of the spiral designs remains a mystery.

Hedge maze at Hever Castle

Hedge mazes

Labyrinths made from hedges have only been around for 400 years or so. By the time they began to appear in the gardens of the stately homes and manor houses of Europe, the ritual significance of the maze had been lost, and they were essentially a frivolous adornment. The maze at Hever Castle in Kent, England, was constructed by William Waldorf Astor in the first decade of the 20th century.

Spirals in the Peruvian desert

MAZE GAMES

The nine men's morris is filled up with mud;
And the quaint mazes in the wanton green,
For lack of tread, are indistinguishable.
Shakespeare, *A Midsummer Night's Dream*

Nine Men's Morris has been popular for centuries. Often played by carving the game's layout into a rock or on turf, and using stones as counters, it bears a remarkable similarity to a shepherd's game played in Wales, called *Trios*, and a Greek game known as *Triothi.*

The popularity of maze games grew in Victorian times and continues today, reflecting our obsession with puzzles of all sorts.

19th-century Mother Goose game

CHARTRES CATHEDRAL

A most famous maze can be found on the floor of the cathedral at Chartres in France. It is about 40 feet in diameter and was probably built in the 13th century. It originally had a metal plate with an engraving of a Minotaur or centaur at its center. The maze is made of blue and white stones, and verses of the *Miserere* psalm are engraved on the white path. The maze was used as a path of penance, the full course of 150 yards to be completed on the knees or barefoot, while repeating prayers.

Penitent monks

Some researchers have conducted tests on the maze using a Geiger counter and other special equipment. Vibrations of earth energy, well above normal, are claimed to have been found inside the labyrinth. If their findings are correct, walking around the maze may well have had an inspiring, invigorating effect on the many barefoot penitents. Mazes of similar design can be found in several medieval European churches and cathedrals, such as those in Lucca, Ravenna, and Rome in Italy, and St. Quentin and Bayeux in France.

Following the path of the pilgrims

This is the ancient and famous maze at Chartres cathedral. Try tracing it yourself. Start on the outside with your finger on the white path, and continue all the way around until you reach the center.

The Candelabra
This unusual design is carved in a hill of dry sand on the coast of the Paracas Peninsula in Peru, not far from the desert lines between Nazca and Palpa. It is more than a thousand years old.

PATTERNS IN THE LANDSCAPE

Megaliths, mazes, and monumental constructions of wood, earth, and stone are not the only legacy of the ancient builders. Our ancestors also imprinted complex patterns of lines on the landscape; these remain among the deepest mysteries of the ancient world.

HERE IS NOWHERE BETTER to study landscape lines than in North and South America. The most famous are on the desert plains between Nazca and Palpa, Peru, in the foothills of the Andes. Hundreds of lines, varying in width, spread across about 200 square miles of desert. At least 1,500 years old, they cut straight through gullies and up hills without deviation, converging at mounds known as ray centers. In places they develop into geometric figures or vast images of birds or beasts — including lizards, monkeys, spiders, and whales.

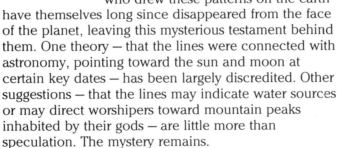

Nazca monkey figure

We know how the lines were created: the dark, oxidized desert surface was removed to reveal a lighter subsoil. But no one knows why they were made. The Nazca Indians who drew these patterns on the earth have themselves long since disappeared from the face of the planet, leaving this mysterious testament behind them. One theory — that the lines were connected with astronomy, pointing toward the sun and moon at certain key dates — has been largely discredited. Other suggestions — that the lines may indicate water sources or may direct worshipers toward mountain peaks inhabited by their gods — are little more than speculation. The mystery remains.

Lines across the Americas

Although the Nazca lines are the most famous in the world, they are far from unique. At sites across the Americas, ancient lines radiate over the landscape. In Bolivia, for instance, there are lines that are even more extensive than those at Nazca, and along them the local Indians have placed their holy shrines. The Incas also had a system of lines, called *ceques*, that radiated out from their imperial city, Cuzco in Peru. These *ceques* are usually traceable in the city because roads have been built along them. But until recently, the *ceques* could only be traced outside the city by following the alignment of the shrines dotted along

Stepping off a precipice
Wide steps have been cut into the rock face where the Anasazi roads meet Chaco Canyon.

THE DIRECT ROUTE

An odd feature of the landscape lines traced by the Anasazi (a name meaning "ancient ones") is their indifference to the lay of the land. In many cases they press on across mountains and ravines as if precipitous drops and sheer rock faces did not exist.

For instance, when an Anasazi road in New Mexico comes off the high mesa, striking the bare rimrock of the Chaco Canyon, it continues in a straight line, its course marked with edging stones. Where it comes to the top of the canyon walls, steps lead straight down to the canyon floor.

Stairs of the gods?

These rock stairs, shown above, are far too wide and steep to have been used for the practical purposes of travel or trade. Elsewhere in the canyon there are narrower steps with handholds, that presumably were used for everyday transportation.

One possible explanation for building such impractical straight roads is that they were symbolically intended for use by the Anasazis' gods.

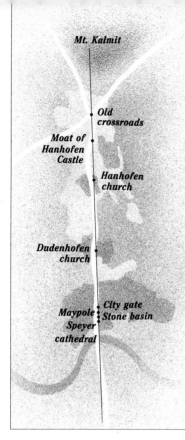

A CLASSIC LEY

Researcher Ulrich Magin has discovered a nine-point ley running for 17 miles on a west-east line from Mount Kalmit to the cathedral in Speyer, Germany. After the mountain, it passes through a crossroads, which dates it at least to medieval times. Next on the line is a square moat where Hanhofen Castle used to stand, followed by the churches of Hanhofen and Dudenhofen.

Direct line to the cathedral

The ley then enters Speyer via the *Altpörtel*, the 13th-century city gate. This gate is linked to the cathedral by Maximilianstrasse, a road once used by German emperors for their triumphal entry into the city, and which directly follows the line of the ley.

A maypole on this street, a survival from pagan times, also falls on the line, as does the most ancient part of the cathedral. This is the *Domnapf*, a huge stone basin in the courtyard, which was filled with wine for the citizens on the consecration of each new bishop of Speyer.

their path. But now they have become visible: they can be clearly seen in aerial photographs that use infrared film.

In North America the Miwok Indians (now extinct) made perfectly straight tracks that ran for dozens of miles through the California sierras, from one mountain peak to another. Farther to the southeast, the Anasazi (a name meaning "the ancient ones" given to an extinct culture by the Navajo Indians) had neither horse nor wheel, yet built perfect 30-foot-wide main roads with equally exact tributary roads just half that width. These systems of straight roads, more than 1,000 years old, radiate around Chaco Canyon in New Mexico. They are difficult to see on the ground, usually appearing as shallow depressions, but since the 1980's aerial photography has identified about 500 miles of such roads; their full extent has still not been plotted. On the northern rim of Chaco Canyon, the Great North Road meets the ruined Anasazi ceremonial center of Pueblo Alto. Archeologists have suggested that this center was a focal point of the roads, which implies that they were themselves sacred.

In the Old World, with its denser population and long history of civilization, it is more difficult to find

"A fairy chain, stretching from mountain peak to mountain peak, as far as the eye could reach."

Idealized ley line

This illustration gives an impression of the kind of markers — churches, hilltops, stone circles — that make up an ideal alignment on the British landscape.

still-visible ancient landscape lines. But the existence of such lines in the past can be deduced from the alignment of sacred sites and other major landmarks. On the island of Java in Indonesia, for example, there is a line of Buddhist temples (including the famous Borobudur) many miles long, along which an annual ceremonial procession occurs. In Cairo, Egypt, as many as 14 mosques and Islamic tombs have been found to align with each other. Lines linking churches, natural features, and ancient sites have been well documented throughout Europe. Some of the more obvious of these alignments, where straight landscape lines pass through many ancient sites, have been termed "leys," and are now accepted by archeologists as intentional, rather than the product of chance. But as in the Americas, their exact purpose remains unclear.

The modern awareness of leys and other land-scape lines is due mainly to Alfred Watkins, who published his classic work *The Old Straight Track* in 1925. On a hot summer afternoon in 1921, he was riding on horseback through the beautiful countryside on the border between England and Wales, an area he

Stone rows
The Merrivale stones on Dartmoor in the southwest of England were laid in a double row, and are more than 2,000 years old.

ALFRED WATKINS

It was Alfred Watkins who coined the term "ley." During fieldwork, he encountered distinctive boulders that he called "mark stones," and he was convinced that they had been set in place by the original surveyors of the lines thousands of years before.

Hilltops, too, were involved in the alignments. Many were crowned with prehistoric earthworks. He called such hilltops "initial points" and claimed that they were used like the sights on a rifle barrel to set the course of a ley.

Religious tradition

Old churches also fell on his leys. At first glance, this seems difficult to explain, as the alignments were supposedly set down in prehistory, long before Christianity existed.

But Watkins correctly pointed out that it was the policy of the early Christian missionaries to reuse pagan sites where appropriate; so they would have built their churches on traditional holy sites of the pagan past. There are numerous examples in Europe and South America of churches occupying prehistoric religious sites.

Other ley markers recognized by Watkins included river fords, holy wells, ancient crossroads, and indentations in the skyline produced by a dip in a line of hills or mountains.

---

had known and loved for many years. He reined to a halt on a high hilltop and took out a detailed map of the country spreading out below him. Noticing that the prehistoric sites on the map fell into straight alignments, he was suddenly overwhelmed by a vision that struck him, he later recalled, like "a flood of ancestral memory." It was a vision of straight lines across Britain, linking ancient burial mounds, stone circles, churches, hilltops, and crossroads, each like "a fairy chain, stretching from mountain peak to mountain peak, as far as the eye could reach...."

Despite Watkins's deep mystical intuition about the importance of the system of leys he had discovered, he rationalized them as being the remnants of a system of traders' straight tracks, initially sighted across the country in the Neolithic period, and marked by mounds and stones. He conjectured that these old straight paths were maintained with modifications until they fell into obscurity some time after the Roman occupation of Britain 2,000 years ago.

City gate
The view through the Altpörtel follows the line of the ley up Maximilianstrasse directly to Speyer cathedral.

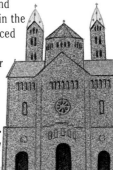

Alfred Watkins

German Holy Lines

German researchers contemporary with Watkins came up with similar findings in their own landscape. Pre-eminent among these were Josef Heinsch and Wilhelm Teudt. Teudt called his lines *Heilige Linien* (Holy Lines).

Dudenhofen church

City gate

Maypole

Stone basin

Speyer cathedral

"The Death of a Chief"
This modern painting by Peter Szumowski is said to illustrate the lines of spiritual energy that radiate across a landscape scattered with ancient Indian burial monuments.

Undeterred by the scorn of professional archeologists, Watkins continued with map and field work, and ley photography, until his death in 1935. Interest in his work then dwindled for a number of decades, until the 1960's, when there was an enthusiastic revival of ley hunting.

Under the influence of the exuberant mysticism of that psychedelic decade, all kinds of exotic additions were made to Watkins's ley theory. With the application of a little imagination, enthusiasts projected alleged leys across hundreds of miles, and even across continents, linking the pyramids of ancient Egypt with the stone circles of England. A myth grew up that Watkins had first seen leys as glowing lines of energy. All sorts of investigators set out with a variety of divining equipment and electronic detectors — or simply applying their own psychic powers — to plot these magnetic "energy lines" across the landscape. The ley craze also became linked to UFO sightings. Writers such as Aimé Michel and Tony Wedd claimed that UFO's

appeared chiefly along leys, which in some way were supposed to attract and direct the extraterrestrial visitors' spacecraft.

Such theories have lost much of their appeal in more recent years. Few serious researchers will now accept the notion of leys extending to a continental scale, and the supposed magnetic forces have proved elusive to measurement. Yet continuing research in countries all around the world — in Israel, Egypt, Japan, China, Indonesia, Cambodia, Germany, France, Britain, and particularly in North and South America — has produced more and more evidence of alignments that fit the definition of a ley as originally outlined by Alfred Watkins.

Indian snake pattern
This boulder design can be found in Death Valley National Monument in southern California.

A universal pattern

It appears that Watkins had perceived the remnants of a deep and universal pattern. But although there are almost as many theories as there are claimed alignments, we still cannot be certain what the ancient builders had in mind when they began their work. It could be that the ancient peoples possessed a spiritual view of the earth that contemporary research simply cannot fathom. Until we begin to learn more about their worldview, the significance of these patterns in the landscape will remain shrouded in mystery.

Viking burial site
At this site at Nørresundby, Denmark, 628 stones mark the graves of warriors; 200 of these form the outline of a huge ship.

THE DRAGON'S PATH

To the present day, the Chinese believe that the landscape, like all living things, manifests energy, known as ch'i. ***This energy flows like a river along the "paths of the dragon."***

THE ANCIENT Chinese art of divining lines of energy in the landscape is known as *feng-shui*. The flow of energy is like the flow of water, which can be encouraged or inhibited by buildings or by features of the landscape. *Ch'i* flows along the paths of the dragon, or *lung mei*.

The flow of energy is stronger in some places than others, and this has important implications for human activities. If the energy flow is too weak at the site of a building, then the structures will lack support and the activities performed there will be sluggish. If, however, the flow is too strong, then the energy force will be dangerous and overpowering.

Avoiding the Secret Arrow

Practitioners of the ancient art of *feng-shui*, known as geomants, still dictate the siting of buildings. Few Chinese would care to build without first having consulted such an expert. If the existing landscape creates unfavorable conditions, then in theory the landscape can be altered to improve the energy

flow. Otherwise, obstacles such as fountains or screen walls, which deflect *ch'i*, are carefully sited to protect the newly constructed building.

Energy flow along an uninterrupted straight line is generally considered harmful. These conditions create a Secret Arrow, or hyper-accelerated force, dispersing any other beneficial energies. Such an arrangement creates bad *ch'i*, causing endless problems and disruptions, which in another culture might be described as the work of poltergeists or gremlins.

Imperial force

The enormous strength of the Secret Arrow along a straight line is considered favorable only along ceremonial routes to imperial shrines. Even then, the flow of energy is often deliberately interrupted by bridges and pagodas. The straight roads radiating from the imperial Forbidden City in Beijing were an attempt to channel *ch'i* towards the emperor on his golden throne.

Auspicious bank
In Hong Kong, even ultramodern buildings that are not designed by Chinese architects, such as the Hong Kong and Shanghai Bank, are planned according to the principles of feng-shui.

Welfare of the dead
Chinese geomants pay particular attention to the siting of tombs. Unlike the straight rows of graves in Western graveyards, tombs are arranged by the feng-shui *adviser to point in the most propitious direction regardless of the surrounding graves.*

Focusing the ch'i
At the end of this long ceremonial avenue, which leads to an imperial tomb, a gate is positioned to focus the flow of energy rushing along the path created for it.

PRACTICAL LEY HUNTING

Using quite simple equipment and easily learned techniques, amateur ley hunters can make a significant contribution to our developing knowledge of ancient landscape patterns.

Inca leys
Streets have been built along the ley lines, or ceques, *within the city of Cuzco, in Peru.*

NEW WORLD LINES
Most ancient landscape lines in North and South America are only visible from the air, but there are a few places where they can still be seen by observers on the ground. Some traces of ancient Indian tracks have been preserved virtually untouched for thousands of years. They usually appear as depressions in the ground or as lines of boulders, which were used to mark the edges of the road.

From the air
Aerial photography is beyond the scope of the amateur ley hunter, but is used extensively in the ongoing process of charting American leys. Infrared photography is also useful: by highlighting changes in vegetation coloring, it shows up paths that have been regularly trodden over the centuries. The existence of *ceques*, lines connecting shrines and radiating out from the Inca capital of Cuzco, Peru, were confirmed in this way.

Conservation
The remoteness of the American sites, although a problem for the ley hunter, is a blessing in disguise. It is obviously imperative to preserve these ancient markings, and the fewer the visitors, the less likely the lines are to suffer damage. Some sites are officially protected, and you may need permission to visit them. Such information can be obtained from archeological organizations.

THE IDEA OF LEY HUNTING is to identify straight lines that link four or five "markers." The technique is most easily applied in the Old World, particularly in Britain, where centuries of human settlement have littered the landscape with ancient sites that constitute valid ley markers. These include burial mounds, prehistoric stone circles, hilltops, crossroads, ancient settlements, forts, and churches.

The first step is to get a map of the area you want to study; the most suitable scale is 1:50,000 (about 1 ¼ inches to 1 mile). A ley is never likely to be more than 25 miles in length, a distance that can be covered on a single map sheet of this scale.

Spread the map out and examine it for suitable markers. Use a long transparent ruler to see whether four or five of these landmarks align. If they do, draw a line on the map to join them up. Make sure to use a very sharp, hard pencil. The narrower the line on the map, the more accurate the alignment is likely to be.

From mapwork to fieldwork
Before you travel to the potential ley site that you have plotted, it is a good idea to transfer this line onto larger-scale maps of 1:25,000 (2 ½ inches to 1 mile). Also make sure you establish an exact compass bearing for the line.

To embark on work in the field, you will need a compass, binoculars, a camera, and a notebook. The most important requirement is accuracy in both observation and notation. In your fieldwork you will be seeking to check the validity of the landmarks plotted on the map, and searching for other possible sites. Are they, in fact, valid ley markers? Is a particular crossroads sufficiently ancient to form a link in the ley? It is essential to obtain an exact sighting on each geographical feature and to locate it with equal accuracy on the map. Take a photograph of each ley marker and, if possible, one that shows the relationship of one landmark to another on the ley (this is surprisingly difficult to do).

Follow-up research
Note down basic details such as the type of land and features of the surrounding landscape. And remember to follow up your expedition by obtaining information about the sites you have plotted and the neighboring area from local libraries and archeological groups.

ST. BARTHOLOMEW'S CHURCH & HYDE GATE

WINCHESTER CATHEDRAL

ST. CATHERINE'S HILL

Winchester ley, England
With its dense concentration of ancient sites, Britain offers classic locations for ley hunting. The Winchester ley is about eight miles long. It passes through six markers, starting north of Winchester at Tidbury Ring, the site of a prehistoric camp. Four miles farther on, near Wonston, is a long mound, or ancient burial earthwork. The ley continues to Winchester itself, site of a pre-Roman settlement, and an important medieval city. The line passes through the 12th-century St. Bartholomew's Church and Hyde Gate, built on the site of Hyde Abbey, where King Alfred the Great is supposedly buried. It continues through the Lady Chapel of Winchester cathedral, and ends south of the city at St. Catherine's Hill, where there are the remains of an ancient camp and a turf maze.

Lost Cities
of the Americas

Central and South America are scattered with impressive remnants of the Indian empires that came to an end with the Spanish conquest of the 16th century. The Mayas, Incas, and Aztecs all raised mighty palaces and temples, and adorned them with paintings and artifacts of gleaming splendor. These sites were the scene of magnificent, but mysterious and bloody rituals, by which homage was paid to the myriad gods who oversaw every aspect of life on earth.

Olmec greenstone statue

Olmec culture

It is generally agreed that the roots of Mayan culture go back to the earlier Olmec civilization, which appeared on the shores of the Gulf of Mexico around 1500 B.C. The Olmecs were especially noted for their skill in sculpting monumental stone heads and for their exquisite jade carving. This greenstone statue depicts a young man holding an image of the "werejaguar" — the chief god of the Olmecs — who combines the features of a large feline with those of a human baby.

The Pyramid of the Soothsayer

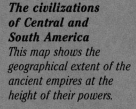

The civilizations of Central and South America
This map shows the geographical extent of the ancient empires at the height of their powers.

KEY	
	The Aztec empire
	The Mayan empire
	The Inca empire

Funeral pottery

Much of what we know about the Mayan religion comes from their legacy of funerary pottery, vessels that they buried with their dead. A good example is this magnificent ceremonial vase, dating from the 10th or 11th century. The intricate patterns commemorate a disastrous flood that the Mayas believed was caused by a malevolent spirit.

Mayan vase

MAYAS

The ruins of Palenque

The civilization of the Mayas originated some 3,500 years ago in the Yucatan Peninsula of modern Mexico and in parts of what are now Guatemala and Belize. The Mayas built large cities centered on massive stone temples that were powerful symbols of the religion that suffused every aspect of their life.

Mayan craftsmen created beautiful pots, vases, carvings, jewelry, and illustrated books. They were skilled mathematicians and astronomers; they evolved their own writing and a calendar that was as accurate as any that we use today.

Mayan civilization went into decline from about A.D. 900 and was eventually destroyed by the Spaniards in the 16th century.

A sacred city

The city of Palenque, Mexico, was at its most magnificent in the seventh century. As the westernmost point of Mayan territory, and therefore the place where the sun "died," it was considered an especially sacred site.

Jade carving

This fine Mayan death mask owes much to Olmec traditions. It was made from more than 200 pieces of jade, the whites of the eyes are made of shell, and the irises and pupils of obsidian. It covered the face of a Mayan chieftain whose remains were found in the sarcophagus of a seventh-century tomb in Chiapas, Mexico.

Mayan pyramid

Even though they are in ruins, there is no mistaking the astonishing architectural sophistication of the Mayan buildings. This sheer-sided structure is known as The Pyramid of the Soothsayer, and can be found at Uxmal, Mexico. Courts, temples, and pyramids such as this were used for religious ceremonies.

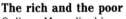

A dangerous game

A ball court was built in every major ceremonial center. The one shown below, in Monte Albán, Mexico, dates from A.D. 775. The game was known as *pok-a-tok*, and was played with a hard rubber ball. The objective was to strike the ball through a hoop projecting from the wall. The victor could become a hero overnight, while the loser could pay with his life. Spectators wagered their jewelry, clothes, houses, even their concubines on the outcome, and were sometimes forced to sell themselves into slavery in order to pay their debts.

Chieftain's death mask

The rich and the poor

Ordinary Mayas lived in small wooden or adobe thatch-roofed houses and worked long hours in the fields. Aristocrats, like the one depicted here, lived in style and wore elaborate clothing, headdresses, and earrings.

Statue of an aristocrat

Pok-a-tok ball court

Mixtec mosaics

Mosaic was a Central American specialty, the most accomplished practitioners being craftsmen of the Mixtec tribe. Rare and precious materials were used in great numbers. This exquisite knife handle, depicting a crouching man, may well have been used in human sacrifices.

Sacrificial knife

AZTECS

The Aztecs settled in Mexico in the 12th century. By the 15th century they ruled the largest empire ever known in Central America. Their capital, Tenochtitlan, was captured by Spanish conquistadors in 1521 and razed to the ground; Mexico City was built on its ruins. The society was full of contradictions: human sacrifice was considered essential, yet in other ways the civilization was advanced, with impressive achievements in engineering, architecture, and sculpture. One magnificent artifact that has survived is a calendar known as the Stone of the Sun, originally found in the Temple of Huitzilopochtli in Tenochtitlan.

Calendar stone

Ancient Aztec city

Teotihuacan was in ruins even in Aztec times and was revered as a place of mystery. For the Aztecs it was "the place of the gods" to which they made pilgrimages. The Pyramid of the Moon was built of bricks faced with stone, and was a spectacular building standing 200 feet tall at one end of the Avenue of the Dead.

Sacrificial rites

The Aztecs worshiped many gods, including the supreme Huitzilopochtli, the sun god and god of war; Quetzalcoatl, the feathered serpent god; and his brother, Tezcatlipoca, the god of chance and fortune. People and animals were sacrificed daily to the gods. Once a year, when Tezcatlipoca was honored, a young man representing ideal beauty was picked to personify him, and was sacrificed in his name. The man's heart was torn out and his head displayed on a skull rack in front of the temple.

The Pyramid of the Moon

Divine powers

The Aztecs believed their stone figures to be imbued with a divine power. The invading Spaniards understood this and, to protect the Catholic faith, destroyed or buried every statue they found. This enormous figure of the earth goddess Coatlicue, some eight feet tall, once stood in a temple in Tenochtitlan. She has two rattlesnake heads and a necklace of human hearts and severed hands, with a skull for a centerpiece.

Skull rack

Stone earth goddess

INCAS

The Inca civilization originated near Cuzco in Peru in the 12th century. By 1500 the Incas' territory extended from present-day Ecuador in the north to Chile in the south. The Incas were not the only civilization in this area. They were preceded by the Nazcas in southern Peru (A.D. 200–600), and lived at the same time as the Chimu people, whom they conquered in 1470.

Although they had no paper, or system of writing, the Incas built impressive palaces, temples, and roads. Inca metalworking skills were highly developed, and their ceramics and textiles were elaborate and beautiful.

Chimu burial mask

Precious metal
For the Incas, gold was "the sweat of the sun." Because of its divine origin, it was reserved for religious use, such as in temple ornaments, and for the adornment of the emperor and the most important members of the nobility. This 13th-century Chimu burial mask is made of embossed sheet gold and was originally painted red, a sacred color in ancient American funeral rites.

Inca doll

Cotton as precious as jade
The Incas buried their dead with the tools they had used during their lifetimes. This burial doll, made from cotton and reeds, was found with the body of a child. The use of humble materials did not make the work of art any less precious. To the Incas all materials were equally expressive of religious truths.

Sea harvest
The waters of the Pacific helped to feed the ancient Indian societies of coastal South America in more ways than one, since fish was used both as a food and as agricultural fertilizer. Sea creatures were prominent motifs in ceramics, paintings, and murals. One example is this wall at the Chimu capital of Chan Chan in northern Peru. In 1400 Chan Chan, with a population of about 50,000, was the largest city in South America.

Nazca pot with fisherman and net

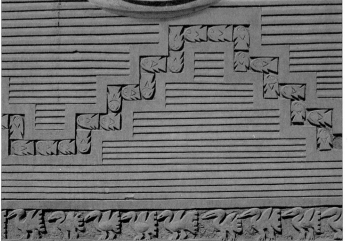

Adobe wall at Chan Chan

Nazca hummingbirds
The images of the ancient Indians of South America reflect the importance in their lives of birds and animals, certain of which had special significance. The Nazcas, forerunners of the Incas, scraped spectacular line drawings out of the landscape of the arid coastal plains around A.D. 500. This long-billed hummingbird is so massive that it cannot be seen at ground level, supporting the contention that such "earth pictures" were intended for the eyes of the gods. The hummingbird also featured in the patterns on Nazca pottery.

Nazca earth picture

Nazca pot with hummingbird motif

LINES AND LIGHTS

For centuries strange light shows — glowing orbs, flickering or floating beams, bright flashes — have been reported at sacred monuments and sites around the world. Are they connected with faults in the earth's crust?

HE EERIE ERODED LANDSCAPE of the Pinnacles National Monument in southern California was the setting for a peculiar play of light in the spring of 1973. At dusk David Kubrin and his wife were heading back to their car after a visit to the monument when they saw an oval of golden light streaking at speed just above the treetops. It swirled around and came to a sudden halt, near enough to photograph. As the holder of a doctorate in the history of science, Kubrin was struck by the fact that the behavior of the light clearly violated the laws of physics. When in motion, it produced shock waves in the air, suggesting that it must have a certain mass. Yet it stopped instantly, suggesting that it was weightless. Any object of mass would have had to decelerate before stopping.

Geological factors

Such earth lights, or "spook" lights as they are better known, have long been observed in different parts of the world. That they really exist is beyond serious doubt. But what could they be? And why do they

Light site
Castlerigg in Cumbria, England (left), is famous for its earth light manifestations. This dramatic visualization (right) is based on a sighting by T. Sington in 1919.

occur where they do? One possible explanation lies in geology. The Pinnacles National Monument site is bounded on the east by the erratic San Andreas Fault, a fracture in the earth's crust where the Pacific and North American tectonic plates meet. It has been suggested that the lights at this location may have something to do with stress on the earth's rock formation caused by seismic activity – the same disturbances that produce earthquakes and volcanoes.

The ancient connection

Along the line of another geological fault lies the ancient stone circle at Castlerigg in Cumbria, England. Here, too, there have been numerous reports of mysterious lights. It is possible that these lights may have been observed by the ancient inhabitants of the

"We then saw a number of lights in the direction of the Druidical circle. Whilst we were watching, one of the lights came straight to the spot where we were standing; at first very faint, as it approached the light increased in intensity. When it came close it slowed down, stopped, quivered, and slowly went out."

Description of earth lights at Castlerigg, by T. Sington, 1919.

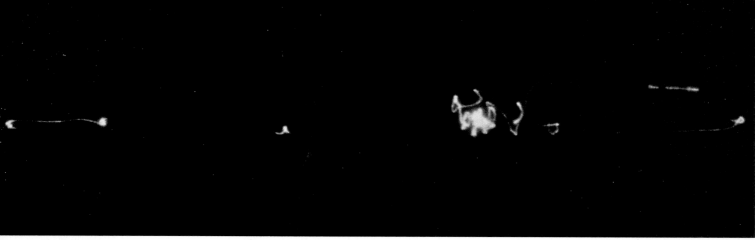

MARFA LIGHTS

For more than a century Marfa, Texas, has been one of the best locations for the appearance of unexplained light phenomena.

One of the most impressive Marfa sightings occurred in March 1973, when two geologists, Pat Kenney and Elwood Wright, chased a couple of lights, first in a jeep and then on foot. They failed to catch up with the phenomena, and recorded their distinct impression that the light had been toying with them. "It was a heck of a lot smarter than we were." Wright told a reporter.

Tourist attraction
This sign can be seen on Highway 90, seven miles east of Marfa.

MARFA LIGHTS
THE MARFA LIGHTS, MYSTERIOUS AND UNEXPLAINED LIGHTS THAT HAVE BEEN REPORTED IN THE AREA FOR OVER ONE HUNDRED YEARS, HAVE BEEN THE SUBJECT OF MANY THEORIES. THE FIRST RECORDED SIGHTING OF THE LIGHTS WAS BY RANCHER ROBERT ELLISON IN 1883. VARIOUSLY EXPLAINED AS CAMPFIRES, PHOS-PHORESCENT MINERALS, SWAMP GAS, STATIC ELECTRICITY, ST. ELMO'S FIRE, AND "GHOST LIGHTS", THE LIGHTS REPORTEDLY CHANGE COLORS, MOVE ABOUT, AND CHANGE IN INTENSITY. SCHOLARS HAVE REPORTED OVER SEVENTY-FIVE LOCAL FOLK TALES DEALING WITH THE UNEXPLAINED PHENOMENON.

area, and, being taken for a mystic or a religious sign, were the reason for siting the stone circle there. If there is a link between earth light phenomena and ancient sacred monuments, it may explain the findings of recent research

> "Fluffy balls of orange-colored fire, moving through space, unhurried and majestic — truly a fitting manifestation of divinity."

that shows that many such monuments are built near lines of geological faulting. The famous ancient Greek oracle at Delphi, for instance, was sited on a fault; fumes issuing from the earth's crust may have been responsible for the prophetic trance of the Delphic priestess. In the U.S.A., the 2,000-year-old Ohio Serpent Mound is situated on top of a crypto-volcanic area that is the only region in North America where geological faults are highly concentrated. Machupicchu in Peru is yet another example of one of the many fault-located sacred monuments around the world.

Sacred locations

There is strong evidence that earth lights have at times been attributed a religious significance. At Sorte Mountain, Venezuela, for example, native shamans look for favorable energies in the form of lights before conducting rituals.

In the western mountains of China, 8,000 feet up, lies Wutai, sacred to Tibetans, Chinese, and Mongols. Amid the peaks in the plateau sits a collection of 300 temples, that may well have been the inspiration for the fabled paradise of Shangri-la. One temple was built by the Buddhists on the southern pinnacle to allow observation of the Bodhisattva Lights. In 1937, the writer John Blofeld witnessed this phenomenon and described "fluffy balls of orange-colored fire, moving through space, unhurried and majestic — truly a fitting mani-festation of divinity."

Accounts of lights at ancient sacred sites are only just beginning to be compiled systematically. Lights have

Mount Shasta
As the sacred mountain of several California Indian tribes, Mount Shasta has been the site of strange light phenomena over a long period of time.

been seen near the great henge circle at Avebury in England, where, in the summer of 1989, orange balls of light were seen to descend into a local field.

In the U.S.A. during the 1970's, lights were seen by trained observers and photographed on the Yakima Indian reservation in Washington. The reservation is adjacent to the Cascade Range, which includes Mount Shasta, a peak that is sacred to all the local Indian tribes. This is also where pilot Kenneth Arnold saw the "flying disks" in 1947 that started the "flying saucer" craze. There is speculation that Arnold's "disks," and many other UFO sitings, may have been earth light manifestations. And there is no question that the Cascades are seismically active, as the eruption of Mount St. Helens in 1980 showed.

Indeed, virtually all earth light reports from across the U.S.A. come from areas of geological faulting. Over 100 locations are known, including Marfa, Texas; Maco Station and Brown Mountain, North Carolina; Ada, Oklahoma; Uinta Basin, Utah; and the Hooker light on the Ramapo Fault near Washington Township, New Jersey.

This still does not tell us exactly what the lights are and where they come from. Research is now starting to reveal that they appear in regions that always contain one or more specific features: geological faulting, a history of earthquake or volcanic activity, mineral deposits, or bodies of water. The lights display electromagnetic behavior — for example, they are attracted to charge collectors such as TV masts, isolated buildings on faults, high-tension cables, and mountain peaks. But they also clearly possess more mysterious properties. U.S. government geologist John Derr has predicted that their study is sure to take us beyond the currently known limits of science.

The Oracle at Delphi
Could escaping subterranean vapors have entranced the priestess before she proclaimed a prophecy to the believer?

PROJECT HESSDALEN

At the beginning of the 1980's, the inhabitants of the remote valley of Hessdalen in Norway reported numerous cases of strange lights appearing in the area. There were blue and white flashes high in the sky, yellow and yellowish-white lights in the valley, and groups of lights moving together near the mountaintops.

When the Norwegian Air Force investigated the phenomena in March 1982, 30 of the 150 inhabitants of the area claimed to have seen the lights. The sightings went back as far as 1944, but locals were reluctant to report them, assuming that they would not be taken seriously. In addition to the reports of the lights, there were also tales of strange noises, "deep booms," and "banging like thunder."

The investigators move in

In June 1983 various UFO groups in Scandinavia formed Project Hessdalen to investigate these phenomena. The original observation period ran from January 21 to February 26, 1984. The team was armed with a wide variety of instruments including: a radar unit; geiger counters; a magnetometer to measure changes in magnetic field; a spectrum analyzer to study radio emissions; a seismograph to measure movements of the earth's crust; and sophisticated photographic equipment.

Their main field headquarters throughout this bitterly cold period, when temperatures dropped as low as -30° F, was a small trailer. Including temporary volunteers, some 40 people were to become directly involved in the project.

The field site
The trailer headquarters of Project Hessdalen was surrounded by instruments set to record any phenomena.

Hard facts

A total of 188 lights were reported during the month the experiment lasted. Although some were definitely identified as aircraft lights, many were not.

Some of the unattributable lights were photographed, and three actually showed up on the radar screen while simultaneously being observed visually. Such "radar-visuals" are highly prized by investigators. In one bizarre case, while the light remained visible throughout, it appeared only on every second radar sweep. The radar tracked another light traveling at a speed of over 19,000 m.p.h.

An astronomer's view

After these findings, it is hard to deny that something strange has been occurring in and around the Hessdalen Valley. Although the phenomena were found to have peaked in 1984, sightings continued to be recorded. The veteran astronomer J. Allen Hynek visited Hessdalen and met the leaders of the project in 1985. His pronouncement was simply: "We have something important in Hessdalen."

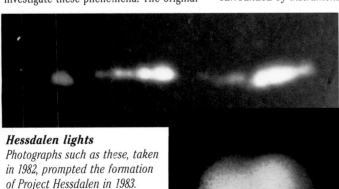

Hessdalen lights
Photographs such as these, taken in 1982, prompted the formation of Project Hessdalen in 1983.

CHAPTER TWO

SECRETS OF THE DEEP

The sea has always held a fascination for humankind. It is vast, ruthless, and unpredictable, and some of the wonders of its depths have proved impenetrable even to modern science. Through the ages, the oceans have been a rich source of myth, legend, and superstition, as well as the scene of real mysteries and unsolved enigmas.

Stories of ghostly apparitions at sea are common. Perhaps it is not surprising that sailors on watch for hours over the immense wastes of the ocean should let their eyes deceive them. But some tales of ghost ships and marine phantoms are not so easily explained away.

On the morning of July 10, 1918, toward the conclusion of the First World War, the U.S. submarine *L-2* was patroling at

Admiral Schroeder
The German commander (shown in the foreground) was forced to order the haunted UB-65 *to be exorcised by a member of the clergy.*

Ghost witness
U.S. submarine of the "L" class at sea in December 1916. It was a submarine of this class that saw the ghostly end of UB-65.

periscope depth off Cape Clear, Ireland, in the eastern Atlantic. Suddenly, her captain, Lt. Paul F. Foster, sighted a target — the lean black shape of a German U-boat lying dead in the water. Clearly marked on the conning tower was the number 65, and to his surprise, he also saw the figure of an officer, arms folded across his chest, standing on the bow.

The U.S. submarine began to maneuver into an attack position, but its torpedoes were not needed. A massive explosion erupted on the *UB-65*, blowing it to fragments. The whole incident had happened so quickly that the watchers aboard *L-2* could hardly believe what they had seen, particularly as they found no wreckage and no survivors. But on July 31, 1918, a terse bulletin issued by German Naval Headquarters confirmed that *UB-65* and its 34-member crew was missing, presumed lost.

And that was the end, or rather the beginning, of one of the most curious mysteries of modern naval history. For the submarine *UB-65* seems to have been haunted during the whole of its brief two-year career.

Built at Bruges, Belgium, in the autumn of 1916, it was one of a batch of 24 U-boats destined for the Flanders Flotilla, and carried a crew of 3 officers and 31 men. It seemed jinxed from the start. Five men were killed during its construction, and just before the first test

dive one man deliberately threw himself overboard. The dive itself was a disaster as the submarine was stuck on the seabed for 12 hours. Back in Bruges, while it was loading supplies for its first operational voyage, a torpedo exploded, killing five enlisted men and a 2nd lieutenant. It was this dead officer who was said to have come back aboard the submarine, to walk the narrow confines of the crew quarters and to stand, arms folded, on the bow.

"We were never a pack of nervous fools," wrote one of the submarine's petty officers, "...we saw the ghost; we never imagined anything. What we saw, we saw, and that was all."

Exorcism ordered

Admiral Gustav N. von Schroeder, the commanding officer at Bruges, ordered that the vessel should be exorcised, but the hauntings continued. The leading gunner, named Eberhardt, committed suicide after seeing the phantom; Petty Officer Richard Meyer followed suit by jumping overboard and swimming out to sea. Finally, when the submarine's commander insisted to Schroeder that he too had seen the ghost, the entire crew was replaced. Just two weeks later, U.S.S. *L-2* watched the submarine's mysterious, violent end.

A German naval psychologist, Professor Hecht, conducted a thorough investigation into the haunting. His report was never published, but he admitted that he could "put forward no alternative theory to the supernatural agency which finally brought about the destruction of this ill-fated vessel."

The *Flying Dutchman*

At least the *UB-65* was a real ship. No one knows for sure whether the phantom vessel known as the *Flying Dutchman* has ever had any material existence. But it has been sighted, and its appearances have been recorded, in all the oceans of the world — on one occasion by a whole squadron of the British Royal Navy.

On July 11, 1881, H.M.S. *Inconstant*, sailing as part of Admiral Lord Clanwilliam's Detached Squadron, apparently encountered the phantom ship in the South Atlantic. On board the

Inconstant were Prince Albert Victor, duke of Clarence, and his brother Prince George, later King George V of England. Their account reads as follows: "At 4:00 A.M. the *Flying Dutchman* crossed our bows. A strange red light as of a phantom ship all aglow, in the midst of which light the masts, spars, and sails of a brig 200 yards distant stood out in strong relief as she came up on the port bow."

Royal cadets
Prince George and his brother Albert Victor.

Suddenly it was gone. Thirteen officers and men, including the commander, saw the fiery ship, and it was sighted simultaneously by the crews of the corvettes *Tourmaline* and *Cleopatra*. As the legend of the *Flying Dutchman* predicts, the sailor who first saw the strange vessel fell to his death from the rigging that very morning.

An equally well-documented and more terrifying sighting occurred on the last day of February 1857, off Tristan da Cunha in the South Atlantic, when the *Flying Dutchman* swept across the bows

---

"A strange red light as of a phantom ship all aglow...came up on the port bow."

---

of the cargo ship *Joseph Somers*. The crew and passengers later gave sworn depositions that they had seen the phantom ship's captain himself, a demonic Dutchman, with "dirty white curls streaming, moon-face a mask of malevolence...." As the ghost vanished, the ship's cargo burst into flames. Those on board were rescued at the last minute by the sailing ship *Nimrod*.

On May 13, 1866, the American sailing ship *General Grant* was wrecked in a vast cavern beneath the cliffs of the

FATA MORGANA

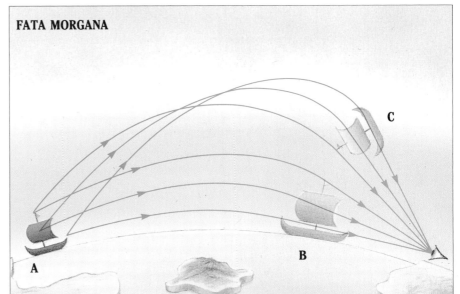

Meteorologists claim that both the mysterious, ghostly Palatine Light seen off Rhode Island and some *Flying Dutchman* sightings can be explained by the phenomenon known as *Fata Morgana*, or "loom of the sea."

This atmospheric effect can distort, magnify, and invert images, in the same way that the sun's heat creates a mirage in the desert or the illusion of shimmering water on the flat surface of a road.

Fata Morgana usually occurs when the sea is much colder than the atmosphere and has cooled the lower layers of the air. The accompanying density changes alter the refractive index of the air and the angle at

which rays of light are "reflected." Objects (like ship A) that are actually over the horizon become visible. The curve of the earth means that the observer cannot really see ship A. But, as the eye expects to receive light in straight lines, the observer "sees" image B and its inverted image C.

Fata Morgana is most common around dawn and dusk, often as a storm builds up. The Straits of Messina, between Sicily and the Italian mainland, are famous for such mirages, which were supposed in local legend to be caused by sorcery. The phrase *Fata Morgana* is the Italian version of the name of the sorceress Morgan le Fay, half-sister of the legendary King Arthur.

Disappointment Islands in the Pacific. This area has been renowned for sightings of ghost ships for at least 300 years. The story goes that the *General Grant* had been pursued for days by a mystery ship that many aboard had thought was the *Flying Dutchman*.

The mystery did not end there. The *General Grant* had been carrying a million dollars' worth of gold dust when it sank. Several salvage attempts were made, all unsuccessful. In March 1870, a salvage party of five men from the schooner *Daphne* entered the cavern...and they were never seen again. Safely back on dry land, the remaining crew of the *Daphne* later reported that,

H.M.S. Inconstant
The Inconstant *almost ran down a phantom ship that was assumed to be the* Flying Dutchman.

♦ PAGE 66

NAUTICAL SUPERSTITIONS

Sailors and fishermen are among the most superstitious people alive. They work in the open and have learned to respect the power of the elements. Over the centuries, seamen have therefore gone to great lengths to avoid giving offense to the gods of the sea, who could unleash the destructive forces of nature.

Umbrellas and cards

Umbrellas and playing cards are usually thought of as taboo at sea. Cards have always been connected with fortune-telling and are known as the devil's picture books. Some say that they should never be taken to sea, others that the tearing up and casting overboard of a pack may produce a favorable change in the wind.

Pig problems

Among Atlantic fishermen, especially in the West Indies, "pig" was traditionally a taboo word. The animal was known instead as Curly-tail, Mr. Dennis, Gruff, Little Fellah, the Grecian, or Turf-rooter. The pig was treated with great respect because it had cloven hooves like the devil, and was the totem beast of the Earth Mother, who controlled the four winds. It was believed that the mention of its name could produce strong winds, and that killing a pig on board ship could bring on a "pig storm."

Left boot

On the east coast of Scotland there is an ancient superstition among fishermen that a left boot is unlucky. If a left boot is trawled up in the nets, it is spat on and thrown back as soon as possible.

Priests and parsons

In most European seafaring nations, clergymen are traditionally unlucky. This may be because early sailors tended to follow Christianity on shore but the pagan gods while at sea. A priest at sea was thought likely to provoke a display of strength by the maritime divinities. In Scottish fishing communities right up to recent times, even to mention the word "priest" was thought to be unlucky. Instead, fishermen used euphemisms such as "gentleman in black," "upstander," or "man in the white collar." If carrying a parson was unavoidable, Scottish seamen took care to wash out their boats thoroughly afterwards.

Light of the moon

There is a superstition that the moon is unlucky. In olden times, sailors would bow to the new moon. They would also try to avoid stepping on, or over, the "moon line" – parts of the deck that were illuminated by the moonlight.

Friday the 13th

"Friday sail, Friday fail" is an old motto of New England fishermen. It was on Friday that the temptation and the banishment of Adam and Eve from the Garden of Eden occurred, as well as the Crucifixion of Christ. Friday the 13th of any month is an exceptionally unlucky day on land and on sea. Even naval vessels have been known to avoid putting to sea on such an inauspicious date.

JULY
13
FRIDAY

...ought but can ne'er
...s Proverb.

64

Eyes

A seafaring tradition of the Mediterranean and the Far East is the painting of "eyes" on each side of the bow of a boat. In ancient China this was believed to help guide the ship. To the ancient Egyptians the eye was that of the gods Osiris or Horus, both of whom prevented harm from black magic. The custom is still followed today on Maltese and Portuguese fishing boats. Even in California, in 1940, the 17,000-ton freighter *Mormacsun* was launched with "lucky" eyes painted on her bow.

TRUSTING TO TATTOOS

In 1771 H.M.S. *Endeavour*, under the command of the explorer Lt. James Cook, visited Tahiti, and a seaman named Robert Stainsby had himself tattooed by a native islander. The craze soon caught on: apart from the names of mothers, wives, and sweethearts, sailors sought to increase their luck with specially designed tattoos. A crucifix on the back was popular, as it was supposed to increase the chances of a Christian burial if the sailor's body washed up on a foreign shore. A guiding star on the hand brought the sailor safely home. A rooster and a pig, one tattooed on each knee, magically ensured that the seafarer never went hungry — he carried with him his own "bacon and eggs."

Right boot

Scottish fishermen traditionally believe that discovering a right boot in their nets is lucky. It is nailed to the mast to bring the boat good fishing and good fortune.

A three-knot wind

According to the 19th-century author Sir Walter Scott, Bessie Millie of Orkney, one of the most northern British islands, sold sailors a charm to end a calm. This cost sixpence, and was simply a piece of string with three knots in it: untying the first brought fair winds, the second brought a gale, while the third knot brought a hurricane.

Human sacrifice

In past centuries the least-valued member of the crew was sometimes sacrificed in the event of bad weather. This was usually the cook! Such customs are not forgotten. In 1930, when the bark *Olivebank* was becalmed in the Atlantic, the crew threw overboard the cook's best pair of pants!

A sacrifice of dignity was also effective: it was said that a storm could be calmed by a woman exposing her breasts to it. This is why ships' figureheads are often of women naked to the waist.

FISHING CHARM

The fishermen of northern France ensure a good catch by hiding brandy in an old bottle below deck, and a cuckolded man aboard (particularly the captain) is especially lucky. Maine fishermen swear by the ritual smoking of tobacco before casting the nets. The fisherman of Dorset, England, also used to deflect evil from witchcraft by hanging a hagstone — a holed stone — over the side of their boats. In Turkey, garlic is kept on fishing boats for the same purpose.

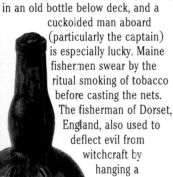

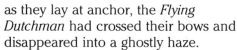

***The* Flying Dutchman**
This illustration from a French magazine of 1911 shows the Flying Dutchman *appearing on the horizon. The two crewmen have good reason to be disconcerted: it is a maritime superstition that the first man to see the phantom ship is doomed.*

Admiral Doenitz
Doenitz was Hitler's commander in chief of submarines in the Second World War. His U-boat crews reported many sightings of phantom ships on their tours of duty east of Suez.

as they lay at anchor, the *Flying Dutchman* had crossed their bows and disappeared into a ghostly haze.

Many other sightings have been recorded. The *Flying Dutchman* was seen twice in Galveston Bay, Texas, in 1892. On the second occasion, the Norwegian ship *Fair Hilda* almost ran aground while desperately trying to avoid it.

The *Flying Dutchman* is not the only ghostly vessel seen on the world's oceans. All down the coast of New England sightings of phantom ships are fairly common. One, regular enough to be a tourist attraction, appears between Christmas and New Year off the coast of Rhode Island in a red ball of fire, similar to that described in the *Inconstant* incident. Known as the Palatine Light, this is alleged to be the ghost of the 18th-century *Palatine*, an immigrant ship deliberately lured ashore by wreckers.

"The men said they preferred facing Allied warships rather than being confronted by a phantom vessel."

Various "natural" explanations for the appearance of phantom ships have been put forward. On the Caribbean island of Carriacou, for example, where sightings of a ghostly white schooner are frequently reported, locals point out a peculiarity of the Leeward Rocks. Approached from one point, they are simple needles of coral; from another they appear as eerily blanched sailing ships, driving toward the shore.

To those who claim to have seen it, the *Flying Dutchman* is real enough. Toward the end of the Second World War, Admiral Karl Doenitz, Hitler's commander in chief of submarines, reported: "Certain of my U-boat crews claim they saw the *Flying Dutchman* or some other phantom ship on their tours of duty east of Suez. When they returned to their base the men said they preferred facing the combined strength of Allied warships in the North Atlantic rather than know the terror a second time of being confronted by a phantom vessel."

THE ORIGINAL DUTCHMAN

No one knows for certain the origin of the *Flying Dutchman* story, but it appears that the name may have been derived from a person, rather than a ship. One candidate for the title was Bernard Fokke, captain of the 17th-century Dutch ship *Libera Nos*, which was renowned for making extremely fast voyages. This ugly and bad-tempered individual was therefore suspected of being in league with the devil. When Fokke did not return from one of his voyages, it was assumed that the devil had claimed his soul.

***Engraving of the* Flying Dutchman**

Vanderdecken

Another well-known version of the *Flying Dutchman* tale concerns a man named Vanderdecken, who captained a merchant ship in the early 1600's. He refused to heave to or shorten sail while rounding the Cape of Good Hope in a storm, despite the pleas of passengers and crew. Lashing himself to the wheel, he continued to drive suicidally into the gale, singing blasphemous songs. For his defiant recklessness, he was sentenced by God to sail on through the storm for eternity.

The Dutchman
A painting of the ghostly Dutch captain by artist Howard Pyle.

THE MARY CELESTE ENIGMA

The disappearance of the crew of the Mary Celeste *in mid-Atlantic is the classic sea mystery. Over a century of speculation has brought us no nearer to knowing the truth.*

James H. Winchester
Winchester was head of the shipping company that owned the Mary Celeste.

URING THE AFTERNOON of December 4, 1872, a 282-ton American brigantine was found rolling in the Atlantic swells some 590 miles west of Gibraltar, seaworthy but with not a soul on board. The derelict's name was *Mary Celeste*, and she was to become a byword for maritime mystery.

The *Mary Celeste* was originally built as the British ship *Amazon* in 1860 at Joshua Dewis's shipyard on Spencer's Island, Nova Scotia. With a length of 103 feet and her brigantine rig, she was similar to dozens of other reliable, medium-sized deep-sea freighters plying the North Atlantic. Sadly there was nothing reliable about the *Amazon*, other than a tendency to catastrophe.

For 10 years she suffered a series of disasters, including two collisions, a fire, and a near-fatal wreck. About 1870 she was bought by James H. Winchester, the founder of a New York shipping consortium. Winchester had her refitted, her hold and cabin remodeled, and her bottom sheathed in new copper. By October 1872 the *Mary Celeste* had been re-registered as an American vessel and was in the East River at Pier 44 in New York City, awaiting her crew and cargo.

The first aboard was the captain, Benjamin Spooner Briggs. He had already held three successful commands with the

The Mary Celeste
The ill-fated vessel soon after she was built.

Winchester company, of which he was a shareholder. A temperate man, he wisely allowed no alcohol on his ship while at sea. Accompanying him on his first voyage in the *Mary Celeste* were his wife, Sarah, and their two-year-old daughter.

By Saturday, November 2, 1872, the *Mary Celeste*'s cargo — 1,701 red oak barrels of denatured alcohol bound for Genoa, Italy — had been loaded aboard. Capt. Briggs went ashore for a final meal with his friend Capt. David Reed Morehouse, master of the British brigantine *Dei Gratia*, which was lying alongside his ship awaiting a cargo.

The Sandy Hook Bay pilot boat towed the *Mary Celeste* downriver to an anchorage off Staten Island, on November 5, where she lay for two days waiting for a break in the weather. Finally, on November 7, 1872, she sailed out into the Atlantic — and into legend.

Adrift in the Atlantic

On November 15, the *Dei Gratia* put to sea with a cargo of petroleum, bound for Gibraltar. At 1:00 P.M. on December 4, at a point about halfway between the Azores and the west coast of Spain, her helmsman spotted a brigantine with tattered sails; it was the *Mary Celeste*.

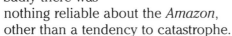

Capt. David Morehouse
Portrait of the captain of the ship that found the Mary Celeste.

Capt. Morehouse eyed his friend's command through a telescope. She had some sails up, but they were unbraced and flapping; nobody was at the wheel.

When there was no reply to his calls, Morehouse sent his first mate, Oliver Deveau, and two seamen to board the stricken vessel. She was totally deserted.

In the mate's cabin a chart showed the track of the vessel up to November 24. The main log, along with the captain's log, sextant, and ship's papers, was missing, and the cradles that had held the ship's lifeboat on top of the main hatch were empty. A strip of railing had apparently been removed to make it easier to launch the boat; everything pointed to the crew having abandoned ship. But why?

A burst barrel

There was damage to some of the sails and rigging, but this appeared to have occurred after the abandonment. One of the pumps had been drawn from the sounding well as if to test how much water there was in the bilges. The water was less than a foot deep — an acceptable level. Plates and cutlery were neatly stowed in the galley, and the beds had been made, though an open skylight had let seawater into the cabin. Rough weather may have been anticipated, because some of the cabin windows were battened with wood.

On deck, two or three of the hatch covers had been removed from the main hold. The cargo was still on board, but the end of one of the barrels of alcohol

Boarding party
Reconstruction of the scene as a boarding party from the Dei Gratia *approaches the deserted ship.*

had burst. Deveau also noticed that the main-peak halyard — a sturdy 100-foot rope — was broken, and a good deal of it was missing. Whatever had happened, it had happened fast. Almost all of the six-month supply of food and water remained on board, and among the many personal possessions left behind were tobacco pipes. A sailor might abandon ship, but rarely his pipe.

Capt. Morehouse ordered Oliver Deveau and the two seamen to patch up the *Mary Celeste*'s rigging. Two days later the brigantines sailed for Gibraltar, arriving on the night of December 12.

The *Mary Celeste* was immediately impounded by Frederick Solly Flood, attorney general for Gibraltar,

THE CAPTAIN AND CREW

Capt. Benjamin Spooner Briggs, 37, had been born into an old seafaring family from Wareham, Massachusetts. He was a religious man and a teetotaler. A contemporary described him as "bearing the highest character as a Christian and as an intelligent and active shipmaster." Briggs's wife, Sarah, accompanied him on this fatal voyage, along with their two-year-old daughter. Sarah shared Briggs's faith, being the daughter of a Congregationalist minister from Marion, Massachusetts.

Friends together

Three of the crew were old shipmates of Briggs; the first mate, Albert G. Richardson, a New Yorker, was married to the niece of James Winchester, the shipowner. Also from New York were the second mate, Andrew Gilling, and the cook-steward, Edward William Head, a Brooklyn man "respected by all." The remaining four crewmen were German: Arian Martens, Gottlief Goodshaad (or Gondshaatt), and two brothers from Schleswig-Holstein, Volkert and Boz Lorensen. These last two had ended up in New York after being shipwrecked and losing all their possessions on a previous voyage. The crew had, of course, been approved by the fastidious Briggs.

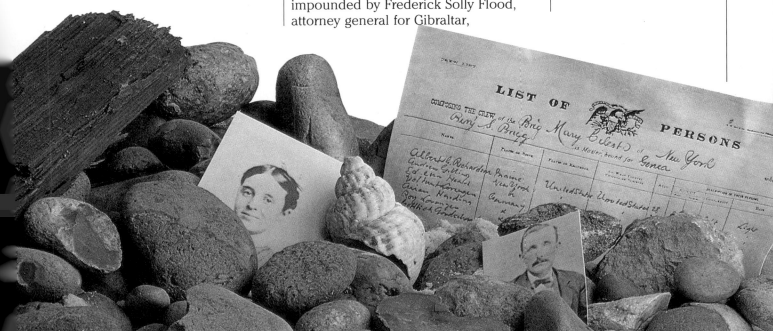

Arthur Conan Doyle

CONAN DOYLE'S *CELESTE*
In January 1884 Arthur Conan Doyle (later to become famous as the creator of Sherlock Holmes) published a short story entitled "J. Habakuk Jephson's Statement" in the *Cornhill Magazine* in London. This referred to the mystery of the *Marie* (not *Mary*) *Celeste*, and provided a fictional explanation for the disappearance of the crew.

Conan Doyle based his story on the character of an American revolutionary named Septimus Goring. The plot involved the hijacking of a ship and the murder of those on board by Goring and accomplices. The ship was finally abandoned off the coast of Africa, hundreds of miles to the south of its intended destination.

Magic talisman
The narrator of the story, Jephson, was the only man spared, on account of a magical talisman he carried. He was allowed to escape by Goring and returned to America to tell his story.

Conan Doyle used the real name of the mystery ship, although slightly changed, as well as several other details supplied by the real-life story of the disappearance. The captain was said to be traveling with his wife and child, and the ship that eventually picked up the derelict was given the name *Dei Gratia.* Apart from these details, "J. Habakuk Jephson's Statement" probably has no more or less truth in it than many other explanations of the tragedy.

who also convened the vice-admiralty court for an inquest into the affair. For the first time in its history no conclusion was reached, but several theories were aired during the hearing.

A drunken frenzy
First, Flood accused some of the missing crew of having murdered the Briggs family in a drunken frenzy before abandoning ship. But it was a "dry" ship, apart from the cargo, and anyone drinking the denatured alcohol would have been crippled by sickness and blinded long before inebriation.

Next, Flood accused Briggs and Morehouse of the crime of barratry (the deliberate defrauding of a shipowner), by rigging the whole mystery, planning it over their supper together the night before Briggs sailed.

This was a gross libel on the known good characters of both captains; apart from that, Briggs owned a one-third share of the Winchester company and would have been defrauding himself by undertaking such a plan.

Flood's third and final explanation was that the crew of the *Dei Gratia* had murdered the crew of the *Mary Celeste* in order to claim the salvage reward. This theory was dismissed by the court. Eventually the inquiry came to a close, and Morehouse and his crew were awarded salvage money. The *Mary Celeste* completed its voyage to Genoa, and was then

sold by Winchester. After a dozen more years and at least as many owners, it was finally wrecked in Chesapeake Bay.

Since then many theories have been suggested to account for the mystery. It will probably never be solved. But one set of circumstances might fit the known facts. Transporting volatile liquids such as alcohol in those pre-tanker days was a risky business, and the hold of the *Mary Celeste*, newly rebuilt and with a copper bottom, must have been almost airtight. A buildup of vapor may have caused one of the kegs to blow its top, which would have made a thunderous noise in that secluded space.

Survival instincts
In such a case Briggs's first reaction would have been to check the bilges to see if the hull had been damaged — hence the drawn pump. Next, with a possible second explosion impending, his instinct may have been to launch the lifeboat to get his wife, child, and the crew out of harm's way, while he stayed aboard alone to investigate. He may have used the main-peak halyard as a line between the lifeboat and the ship.

But at that point a wind may have sprung up, and the brigantine begun to sail away. Unable to handle the ship by himself, Briggs would have tried to climb down the halyard to rejoin the others in the lifeboat. The halyard was either cut or came apart. The overloaded lifeboat was swamped and the *Mary Celeste* sailed on. This story is improbable, but, to quote Sherlock Holmes, when you have eliminated the impossible, whatever is left must be the truth.

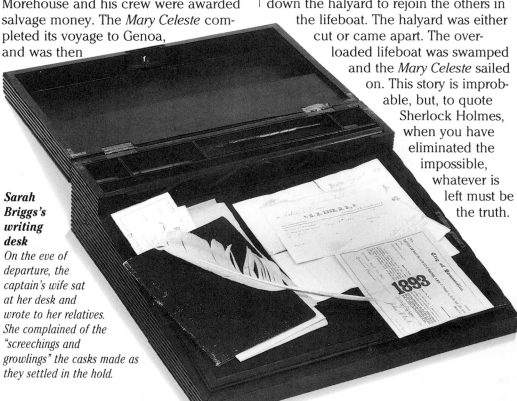

Sarah Briggs's writing desk
On the eve of departure, the captain's wife sat at her desk and wrote to her relatives. She complained of the "screechings and growlings" the casks made as they settled in the hold.

POSSIBLE EXPLANATIONS

Of the many possible solutions to the Mary Celeste riddle that have been suggested, only a few fit the known facts. Some are patently ridiculous, and none of them is wholly convincing.

Mutiny An obvious explanation; but the crew seemed trustworthy, the captain was no tyrant, and there were no signs of a struggle.

Piracy Unlikely. Why would the pirates leave the valuable ship and cargo? Records of the period also show that there were no pirates operating in that area.

Conspiracy Briggs owned one-third of his ship and would have had little to gain by splitting the salvage money with Morehouse. Such a plan seems out of character, risky, and motiveless.

Explosion This is quite likely. The cargo was known to be volatile, and when the ship was found one of the barrels had burst, and the hatch covers were off. Fear of fire or further explosions would help to explain why the crew abandoned ship.

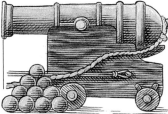

Attack by *Dei Gratia* This seems unlikely in view of the fact that the captains were good friends. And how would the *Dei Gratia* have caught the *Mary Celeste*, which had eight days' head start?

Waterspout If the *Mary Celeste* had been hit by a waterspout, the captain and crew might have panicked and abandoned ship. This certainly would have caused low pressure, which may have drawn water up into the bilges and convinced the crew that the ship was sinking.

Storm or tidal wave This is unlikely. Why would the crew abandon ship and take their chances in a small boat if the *Mary Celeste* was not seriously damaged by wind or wave?

Madness A possible explanation. The captain may have gone quietly insane and ordered everybody into the lifeboat. Or he may have gone berserk, and the crew took to the boat to escape.

Poisoning It has been suggested that a form of fungus called ergot, which can develop on stale bread, may have caused suicidal insanity. However, there was nothing wrong with the food and water found on board the ship.

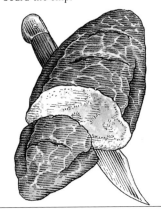

Drunkenness Almost impossible: the cargo of alcohol was the only drink on board and that was denatured, and thus undrinkable.

Sea monster attack This is theoretically possible. If the ship was threatened by a monster squid, whale, or other creature, the crew might have launched the lifeboat to get clear. But it is a highly improbable turn of events.

Abduction by UFO A wildly unlikely theory that has nevertheless attracted a lot of attention in recent years. As a point of detail, it is very improbable that the crew would have launched the lifeboat before being abducted.

THE BERMUDA TRIANGLE

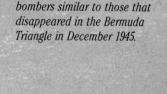

"They vanished as completely as if they had flown to Mars."
Attributed to member Navy Board of Inquiry

ONE OF THE MOST spectacular disappearances associated with the Bermuda Triangle was the loss on December 5, 1945, of six airplanes and 27 men, in two separate incidents. Opinions differ as to whether or not this disaster should be attributed to some mysterious or supernatural force.

The legend of Flight 19
The story usually told differs markedly from the official account. The legend is as follows:

At 2:00 P.M., Lt. Charles C. Taylor took off in good weather with a flight of five U.S. Navy Grumman Avenger torpedo bombers on a training hop over the Atlantic Ocean. In each plane there should have been one pilot and two crew, but one crewman had failed to turn up because, he said, he had had a premonition of danger.

At 3:15 P.M., Taylor radioed the control tower:

Taylor: *This is an emergency. We seem to be off course. We cannot see land....Repeat....We cannot see land.*
Tower: *What is your position?*
Taylor: *We are not sure of our position. We cannot be sure just where we are....We seem to be lost.*
Tower: *Assume bearing due west.*
Taylor: *We don't know which way is west. Everything is wrong...strange....We can't be sure of any direction — even the ocean doesn't look as it should....*

The control tower personnel were puzzled. Visibility was good, and the sun was a sure guide to direction. Taylor had only to fly toward the sun to head west. What was preventing him from seeing the sun? Static and interference made communications progressively more difficult, but the control tower picked up some conversation between the pilots. This included the observation that every gyro and magnetic compass in the planes was "going crazy" — each showing a different reading. Shortly after 4:00 P.M., radio contact ceased.

There was worse to come. A Martin Mariner flying boat with a crew of 13 was immediately dispatched to Flight 19's last reported position. Nothing more was heard from either Flight 19 or the Mariner — apart from a mysterious faint call sign "FT...FT...," presumably from Taylor's plane, FT-28. But this was two hours after the Avengers should have run out of fuel and ditched

Tracing the Triangle
The Bermuda Triangle is situated in the western Atlantic, off the southeast coast of the U.S.A. It is normally defined as the area within a triangle extending from southern Florida to the island of Bermuda, south to Puerto Rico, and then back to Florida. Many disappearances ascribed to the Triangle have actually taken place outside this area; in many other cases it is not known exactly where the ship or plane was lost.

According to the U.S. Coast Guard some 150,000 boats cross the Bermuda Triangle every year. Around 10,000 of these send a distress call. About five losses, on average, are recorded annually.

FLORIDA

Missing Mariner
A Martin Mariner flying boat was lost during the fruitless search for the planes of Flight 19.

Flight 19
A flight of five Avenger torpedo bombers similar to those that disappeared in the Bermuda Triangle in December 1945.

> "The Legend of the Bermuda Triangle is a manufactured mystery...repeated so many times that it began to take on the aura of truth."
> **Lawrence Kusche**
> *The Bermuda Triangle Mystery – Solved*

VICTIMS OF THE TRIANGLE

Most authorities agree that these ships and planes and their passengers and crews have met disaster within or close to the Bermuda Triangle.

Lost or abandoned ships:

1880 *Atalanta*, sail training ship
1925 *Cotopaxi*, freighter
1950 *Sandra*, freighter
1955 *Connemara* IV, yacht
1958 *Revonoc*, racing yacht
1963 *Marine Sulphur Queen*, tanker
1963 *Sno' Boy*, fishing boat
1967 *Witchcraft*, cabin cruiser
1973 *Anita*, freighter
1980 *Mount Horizon*, freighter

Missing aircraft:

1945 Five Avenger bombers; one Mariner flying boat
1947 Superfortress bomber
1948 *Star Tiger*, Tudor IV airliner
1948 DC-3 airliner
1949 *Star Ariel*, Tudor IV airliner
1956 Marlin flying boat
1963 Two KC-135 stratotankers
1965 C-119 Flying Boxcar cargo plane
1967 Chase YC-122 converted glider
1989 DC-3 spray plane

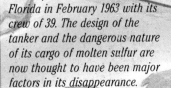

The Marine Sulphur Queen
This ship was lost off the coast of Florida in February 1963 with its crew of 39. The design of the tanker and the dangerous nature of its cargo of molten sulfur are now thought to have been major factors in its disappearance.

into the sea. Despite an enormous air search totaling 4,100 hours and covering 380,000 square miles, no wreckage from the planes was found at the time.

Little basis in fact

In his book, *The Bermuda Triangle Mystery — Solved*, published in 1975, Lawrence Kusche refused to accept that there was anything mysterious about the disappearances. He told an equally gripping story of human error and simple misunderstanding, based on a careful study of the 400-page report of the U.S. Navy Board of Inquiry.

He pointed out that the radio conversations reported in the legend of Flight 19 did not occur. At no stage did Taylor say that everything was "wrong" or "strange," or that the ocean did not "look as it should." The recorded radio transmissions show only that both Taylor's compasses were malfunctioning. The final call sign of "FT...FT...." is attributed to desperate attempts by Miami Radio to contact the flight, rather than, as implied by the sensationalized version, a radio communication from beyond the grave.

A fatal error

The final fix on Flight 19's position shows it to be much further north than Taylor thought, over the Atlantic rather than the Gulf of Mexico. Taylor had only recently been posted to Fort Lauderdale, and Kusche suggests that he mistook Walker Cay in the Bahamas for the Florida Keys. Once lost, his instincts to fly north and east took the planes further away from base. Two poignant radio transmissions from trainee pilots reveal that they had a better idea where they were: "Dammit, if we would just fly west we would get home." As regards the weather, Kusche points out that it was deteriorating fast. The board of inquiry was told that the sea was: "rough and unfavorable for a water landing."

Kusche produces strong evidence that the search plane exploded in the air a few minutes after takeoff at 7:27 P.M., rather than shortly after 4:00 P.M., as the Flight 19 legend implies. The master of the S.S. *Gaines Mills* reported seeing an aircraft explode at the exact position and time that the flying boat disappeared from the radar screen.

Kusche's verdict is that the Flight 19 incident was a double tragedy caused by mechanical failure, human error, and bad weather. A mystery remains, however. Kusche fails to mention the crewman who failed to report for duty, perhaps because he is not mentioned by the board. But if he did exist and he did have a premonition, he may not have been alone. The report confirms that Lt. Taylor himself asked to be excused from leading Flight 19 only 45 minutes before takeoff.

Charles Berlitz

BERLITZ AND THE TRIANGLE

Charles Berlitz is the grandson of Maximilian Berlitz, founder of the famous language schools. His book, *The Bermuda Triangle*, published in 1974, popularized the idea of a deadly region of the ocean into which planes and ships ventured at their peril.

Aliens and Atlantis

Among the theories advanced by Berlitz to explain the number of losses in the area are:
◆ A large magnetic vortex through which a craft and its occupants could slip into a different point in time and space.
◆ The action of aliens from outer space or from inside the earth.
◆ The activation of man-made power complexes on the seabed left by a previous civilization, perhaps the lost city of Atlantis.

The skeptical view

Skeptics have countered by pointing out that the Bermuda Triangle is an area full of natural hazards, especially unpredictable weather. Given the heavy sea and air traffic in the region, the recorded losses may not be remarkably high.

PUERTO RICO

MONSTERS AND MERMAIDS

Sightings of sea monsters and merfolk have been reported in every ocean in the world since the beginning of recorded history.

I N THE EARLY YEARS of the last century, monsters were frequently sighted off the coast of New England. Said one witness in August 1817: "His head was about as long as a horse's and was a proper snake's head...his eyes were prominent and stood out from the surface." Others remarked on the beast's undulating back and said they were certain that what they had seen was neither whale nor shark.

One explanation for such sightings is that people tend to identify what they see in terms of their own knowledge and beliefs. The mythology of the sea has been with us for so long that any unusual object is likely to be described as a sea monster. In fading light, it is possible that a walrus could be mistaken for a merman, or a seal for a mermaid. On the other hand, unknown sea monsters may really exist; certainly the oceans are vast enough to hide almost anything in their unexplored depths.

Jonah in stained glass, France

JONAH AND THE WHALE

The story of Jonah and the whale is one of the most famous and ancient tales of monstrous creatures of the sea.

In the Bible, Jonah was chosen by God to convert the heathens in Nineveh, but he fled from his duty and escaped on a boat. God punished him by sending a terrible storm. When his fellow passengers learned that Jonah was the cause of the storm, they threw him overboard, and he was swallowed by a huge fish. (In later versions of the story this became a whale.)

Swallowed whole

In the belly of the beast, Jonah repented to God, and three days after he had been swallowed, the fish or whale spat him out unharmed.

Over the centuries, the story of Jonah and the whale has been depicted by countless artists, in almost every medium imaginable, from stained glass to mosaic and carved stone.

Armenian Jonah, Lake Van, Turkey

Bronze sea serpent from Denmark

Whale tales

Until the modern scientific age, real creatures, such as whales, were often confused with monsters of myth. Tall stories about encounters with whales abounded. A favorite was the sailors' yarn in which a boat draws up alongside an island in mid-ocean, the crew disembark and light a fire, only to drown when their "island" — in reality a whale — suddenly submerges. Variations on this fantastic tale were widely believed until recent times.

Whale fantasy by artist Julien Menu

Viking visions

Ninth-century Scandinavian craftsmen were inspired by tales of strange creatures encountered by their seagoing countrymen, the Viking marauders, as they sailed the cold waters of the North Atlantic. These elaborately carved wooden heads of sea monsters once decorated objects buried with a Viking queen. They were found at her grave, the Oseberg ship burial.

Viking carving from Oseberg ship burial

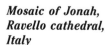

Mosaic of Jonah, Ravello cathedral, Italy

A sinuous serpent

This bronze sea serpent was made in Denmark around 3,000 years ago and formed part of a religious relic known as a cult boat. It has been suggested that sightings of sea serpents might have been based on a glimpse of a line of playful sea otters, their backs bobbing in the waves looking like the curved coils of a long serpent's back.

Pursued by an octopus

Giant octopuses have been sighted in all the world's oceans. Japanese legend has it that the Dragon King rules a magical land beneath the seas, and the sea creatures are his vassals. This 19th-century Japanese triptych illustrates the story of a fisherwoman who steals a jewel from the Dragon King. She is forced to flee from a whole host of sea monsters, among them a giant octopus.

The coils of Midgard

Made in Sweden during the seventh century, this brooch depicts Midgard, the "world serpent" — so-called because it encircled the globe beneath the oceans. In Viking folklore, storms were said to be caused by the writhing of the serpent.

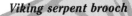

Viking serpent brooch

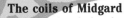

*Ninth-century
Viking carved post*

Here be dragons...

A map made in 1572 by Olaus Magnus depicts the strange and fearsome creatures said to infest the Norwegian Sea. The most famous of these was the Kraken, which was reputed to pluck sailors from the decks of their ships. In modern times, the Kraken has been identified tentatively as a giant squid.

*16th-century
Scandinavian chart*

The mermaid in church
The mermaid was a common subject for craftsmen in medieval churches, usually serving as a symbol of the lures of the flesh. Represented as a beautiful long-haired maiden from the waist up, she usually carries a comb in one hand and a mirror in the other. From the waist down she has the tail of a fish. This mermaid is in Clonfert cathedral, County Galway, Ireland.

Greek plate depicting Triton and Hercules

12th-century mermaid carving

Taken for a ride
Sea monsters and mermaids were often depicted together. A dramatic illustration from the German magazine *Jugend* shows a mermaid with flowing locks riding a serpent across the waves of a foaming sea. A similar theme appears on a 2,000-year-old Greek jewelry box, but in this case a Nereid, or sea nymph, reclines on the back of a mysterious sea creature.

Magazine cover, 1897

Greek silver jewelry box

Monsters of Greek mythology
According to Greek myth, the Mediterranean Sea abounded in other-worldly perils. For example, Perseus spied Andromeda about to be sacrificed to a sea monster. He fell in love with her and saved her life by killing the beast. More decorative but equally dangerous were the Sirens, mermaids whose bewitching voices lured sailors to their deaths. Ulysses told his men to block their ears with wax and chain him to the mast so that he could become the only mortal to listen to their songs and survive.

"The Freeing of Andromeda" by Piero di Cosimo

"Ulysses and the Sirens" by Herbert Draper

Triton versus Hercules

This ancient Greek plate shows the god Triton locked in mortal combat with Hercules, the greatest of the Greek heroes. Triton was a merman, offspring of a mortal mother and Poseidon, god of the sea. Although less well remembered today, mermen were once as common in myth as mermaids.

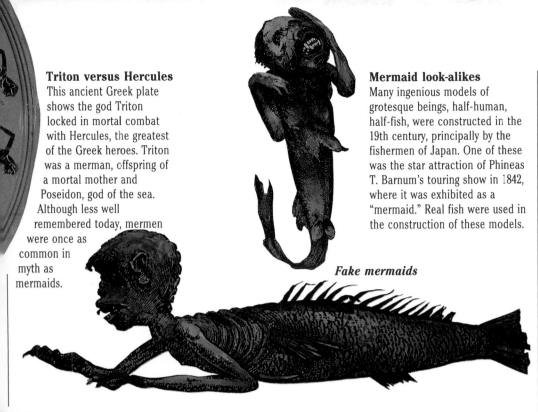

Mermaid look-alikes

Many ingenious models of grotesque beings, half-human, half-fish, were constructed in the 19th century, principally by the fishermen of Japan. One of these was the star attraction of Phineas T. Barnum's touring show in 1842, where it was exhibited as a "mermaid." Real fish were used in the construction of these models.

Fake mermaids

MODELS FOR MONSTERS

Are sea-monster sightings really just fleeting glimpses of such rare creatures as the giant squid, the elephant seal, or the basking shark? Some experts believe so.

A coelacanth

Giant squid

The Kraken, for example, a monster much feared by Norse sailors, may have been inspired by the giant squid, which measures up to 60 feet long.

Basking shark

The huge but harmless basking shark, often seen at the surface, could be mistaken for a monster. In death, its appearance is even more sinister: as parts of the corpse rot, it seems to develop a long, thin neck and four legs.

Lost species

Rare species of giant fish continue to be discovered. The 14-foot megamouth shark was unknown until 1976, while the first coelacanth, thought to have been extinct since the age of the dinosaurs, was caught in 1938. The monsters of legend may yet await us in the sea's mysterious depths.

Double-tailed duo

The way merfolk are depicted varies widely. Two tails are quite common, as in these representations of a 13th-century merman from Berchtesgaden, Germany, and a mermaid on the seashore from a late 15th-century French manuscript.

Merman carving from Germany

Mermaid in French manuscript

Chinese dragons

In Chinese mythology, dragons were good rather than evil. Cloud dragons, such as these from an 18th-century carved red lacquer vase, are also associated with the oceans. On the vase, nine dragons in all are shown pursuing pearls among the clouds.

The serpent's fishwives

In the Hindu legends of India, the wives of the snake Kaliya, who symbolizes death and the underworld, are depicted as fish-tailed spirits, very similar to mermaids in the traditional folklore of the West. Here Kaliya is trodden down by the dancing feet of Krishna.

A monster chart

Early mariners genuinely believed that sea serpents and monsters were as real as crabs, lobsters, seals, and fish. This 16th-century chart shows some of the creatures that were reputed to lurk in distant oceans.

ARKEOLOGY

The story of the Flood and Noah's Ark is one of the greatest sea mysteries. Mountaineers, archeologists, explorers, pilots, and even astronauts have been involved in "arkeology" — the search for the remains of the original ark.

James Irwin
Astronaut turned ark-hunter.

IN 1971, AS HE STOOD on the surface of the moon looking back on the greenish blue orb of the earth through the vastness of space, astronaut James Irwin's thoughts turned to the Old Testament. Like Noah in his ark, Irwin and his fellow travelers had made landfall after a perilous journey. There and then, Irwin vowed that when his NASA days were over he would set out to find the remains of the original ark on Mount Ararat in Turkey.

If such a vow coming from a man of Irwin's scientific background seems eccentric, his obsession was not unique. Many respectable modern archeologists believe that something more than myth lies behind the detailed account in Genesis of Noah's divine mission to build an ark and save selected creatures from the Flood.

The Flood legend

Classical sources too support the story. In Greek mythology, Prometheus annoys Zeus, who decides to drown humankind in a flood. But Prometheus warns his son Deucalion, who weathers the storm in an ark (or chest) with his wife, eventually coming to rest on Mount Parnassus. In the fourth century B.C. Plato added the tale of Atlantis, the drowned continent, while the writer Lucius of the second century A.D. told of a Syrian version of the Deucalion saga. Taken together, these impressive ancient accounts of floods seem to verify each other.

Early 18th-century thinkers took the Genesis version of the story at face value, the only argument being over dates. Dr. James Ussher, an early-18th-century archbishop of Armagh in Ireland, used Old Testament dates and genealogies to arrive at a date of 2349 B.C. for the Flood, compared with 4004 B.C. for the Creation.

Mount Ararat, Turkey

Toward the end of the 18th century, however, advances in geology began to suggest that the world was older

Animal pens
The Bible describes an ark with a cavernous interior. Presumably this was crammed with pens where the animals were tethered.

Wooden construction
According to the Bible, the ark was made of gopher wood, the ancient name for white oak.

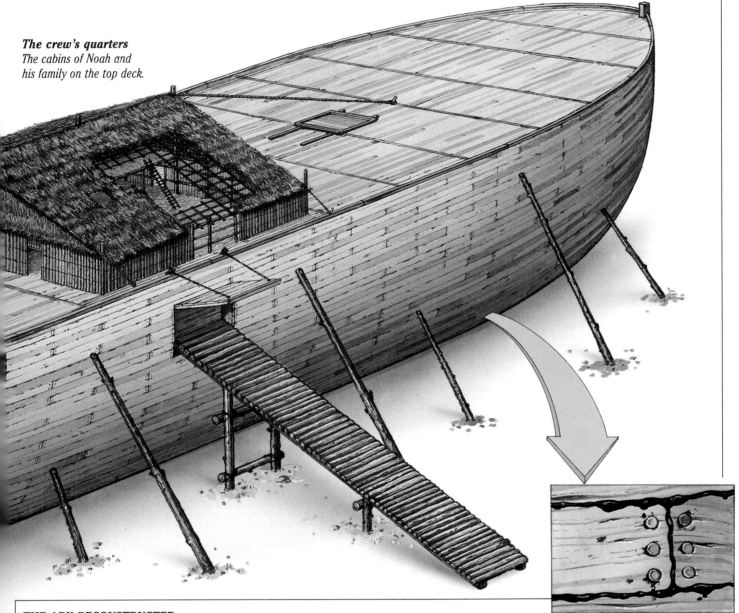

The crew's quarters
The cabins of Noah and his family on the top deck.

THE ARK RECONSTRUCTED

This artist's impression of what Noah's ark may have looked like during its construction is based on the detailed information given in Genesis.

God commanded Noah to build an ark with three stories, a roof, and a door set in one side. Once constructed it was 300 cubits long, 50 cubits across the beam, and 30 cubits tall. The ancient cubit measure equals approximately 18 inches.

A wide gangplank would have been necessary to allow the multitude of animals to enter the ark, and, in order to support the colossal weight of the vessel, wooden scaffolding would have been used to prop up the ark until the flood waters could float it.

Watertight seams
According to the Bible pitch was used to caulk the seams of the ark, both inside and out.

Curved beams
Contemporary craftsmen would have exploited the natural curves of timber to construct the hull.

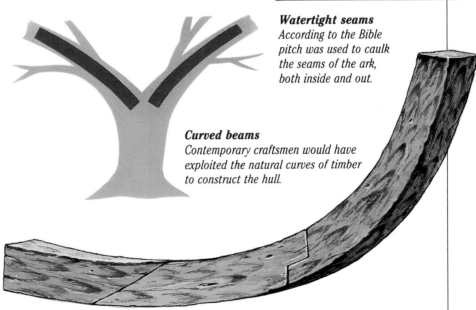

Interlocking joints
The vast curved hull would have required skillful carpentry.

Gilgamesh
The chronicle of this Babylonian hero records the Sumerian flood.

THE SUMERIAN FLOOD
Utnapishtim, a citizen of Shurrupak on the banks of the Euphrates, received warning of the forthcoming deluge in a dream. The god Ea instructed him to build a large boat:
These are the measurements of the bark as you shall build her: let her beam equal her length, let her deck be roofed like the vault that covers the abyss; then take up into the boat the seed of all living creatures.

A week's work
Utnapishtim had the boat built in seven days. It had seven decks in all, with nine bulkheads, and covered an acre in area. Pitch and asphalt were used to make it watertight. Utnapishtim filled it with provisions, and took with him all his family, plus domestic and wild animals, and craftsmen.

After six days of heavy rain and flooding, the boat grounded on Mount Nisir. A week later Utnapishtim released a dove, then a swallow, then a raven. The raven found land and did not return, which was the long-awaited sign that the flood was subsiding.

than either of these dates. The publication of Charles Darwin's revolutionary ideas in *The Origin of Species* in 1859 had a further impact on scientific opinion. Darwin's theories appeared to discredit Genesis as a historical document. He asserted that the species of animals currently existing on earth had been produced not by the Creation, but by evolution.

But the flood story would not go away. As anthropologists studied far-flung cultures in the wake of Darwinism, they found close variants of the Noah story all over the world. India, China, Burma, Malaya, Hawaii, all had their versions of the flood, as did the Aborigines of Australia, the Maoris of New Zealand, and many North and South American Indian tribes, including the Eskimos.

Carved in clay
Then, in the 1870's, came the sensational discovery of the clay tablet library of the 7th-century B.C. king Ashurbanipal at Nineveh on the Tigris, in what is now Iraq. Among the 20,000 inscribed tablets, 12 told the story of the Babylonian hero Gilgamesh and dated from the Sumerian civilization of about 4000 B.C. — very much earlier than either Genesis or the early Greeks. And the 11th of these tablets includes a conversation between Gilgamesh and a man named Utnapishtim, who, like Noah, had built a boat to escape a flood sent by the gods.

Meteorologists were fascinated by Utnapishtim's account of the onset of

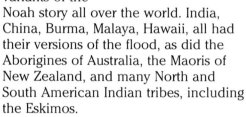

Sir Leonard Woolley on site at Ur

Flood map
The extent of the flood on the Mesopotamian plain.

the deluge, which precisely described what would happen if a cyclone drove the waters of the Persian Gulf over the low lands of Mesopotamia. Particularly moving was the scene of desolation he described after the flood: "I looked at the face of the world and there was silence, all mankind was turned to clay."

So the reality of the flood legends was once more the center of dispute, but with a new twist. Was Noah only a garbled version of earlier tales, or had both he and Utnapishtim been involved in deluges? Had their flood also engulfed the Eskimos, Aztecs, and Aborigines in a single global catastrophe, or had there been a period of deluges all over the world?

It was not until 1930 that the British archeologist Sir Leonard Woolley settled the Mesopotamian flood dispute. Woolley had been excavating the Royal Cemetery at Ur in Iraq, digging straight down and uncovering layer upon layer of artifacts that had been deposited over the centuries. Below these was a thick layer of mud, which had obviously been deposited by water. Far too high to be river mud, it baffled Woolley, who ordered the dig to continue.

After about nine feet, the mud petered out, to be replaced by rubble in which were deposited flint tools and fragments of crudely made pots — an unmistakable Stone Age settlement. Woolley consulted with his colleagues, but there was only one conclusion to be reached. He telegraphed the British Museum: "We have found the Flood!"

Over the next few years similar shafts were sunk over a wide area of the

region. By plotting the thickness of the mud layer, Woolley decided that water had spread inland about 400 miles from the Persian Gulf to a breadth of about 100 miles. "It was a vast flood in the valley of the Tigris and the Euphrates which drowned the whole of the inhabitable land," concluded Woolley; "For the people who lived there, that was all the world."

Could Noah have built a vessel to escape such a catastrophe? According to shipbuilders, archeologists, and geologists, the answer was yes. Neolithic people had the tools, materials, and skills, and the ark described in Genesis would have been perfectly seaworthy.

So the hunt for the ark itself began again in earnest, centering on the volcanic mountain mass of Ararat, a 16,000-foot-high range about 25 miles

Searchers for the ark
Members of the 1984 expedition to Mount Ararat, including James Irwin (left).

long and 12 miles wide stretching between the Caspian and Black Seas, on the border between the Soviet Union, Turkey, and Iran. There were several intriguing though undocumented reports to encourage the new "arkeologists," as those involved in the quest for the ark were called.

Much of Ararat was actively volcanic, and in 1840, after an eruption, Turkish workmen reported seeing the prow of a large ship jutting from a glacier on the mountain slopes. Geologists made the difficult climb, confirmed the find, and were said to have entered three chambers of the ship. In 1893 Dr. Nouri, archdeacon of Jerusalem, rediscovered

the site and stated that he had found the prow and stern of the ship, which was made of thick wood of a dark red color. Deep snow had unfortunately obscured the interior.

In 1914, a Russian fighter pilot named Roskowski reported that he had flown over the remains of the vessel on the southern flank of Ararat. Despite the war, Czar Nicholas II sent a military expedition of 150 men, which found the ship and took photographs and measurements. Sadly their report vanished three years later during the Bolshevik Revolution of 1917.

Ancient hand-hewn timber

More recently, an expedition led by the French explorer Fernand Navarra reported finding what looked like a vessel about 13,800 feet up and sunk in a glacier. The ship was about 450 feet long (roughly the length of the ark described in Genesis) and had sloping sides. Navarra made three expeditions between 1952 and 1955, bringing back pieces of apparently hand-hewn timber of great age, although Carbon-14 dating tests proved inconclusive.

In 1965, the *Daily Telegraph* of London, England, published an aerial photograph of the outline of a boat about 400 feet long. Despite protests from orthodox geologists that the shape was probably a freak glacial formation, several more expeditions, mainly Turkish-American, made the icy climb to find what may or may not be Noah's Ark. The expedition of August 1984 included as one of its members astronaut James Irwin, fulfilling the vow he had made on the moon.

The leader of this expedition, Marvin Steffins, a director of U.S. International Expeditions, brought back fossil samples. He admitted that the real evidence would need long excavations to dig out, but added, "we believe this to be the site."

NOAH'S ARK
God warned Noah that he was going to flood the earth to destroy the wickedness of humanity, and instructed him to build an ark:
Make yourself an ark of gopher wood; make rooms in the ark, and cover it inside and out with pitch....the length of the ark three hundred cubits, its breadth fifty cubits, and its height thirty cubits....with lower, second, and third decks. Genesis 6:14 – 16
God told Noah to fill the ark with provisions, and at least two of every species of living creature on the earth, as well as his sons and their wives.

A hard rain falls
When God sent the rain, it went on for 40 days and nights, and the Flood bore the ark away. All the mountains on earth were covered, and every living thing died, except those on the ark. The Flood lasted 150 days.

When the waters began to recede, the ark came to rest on the mountains of Ararat. Noah sent out a dove, to see if the land had dried out. The dove returned with a leaf from an olive tree. On its second flight it did not return at all — so Noah knew that the Flood was over.

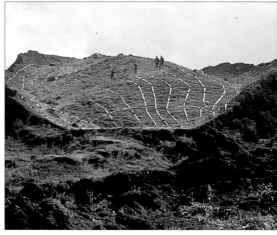

Timbers of the ark?
Traces of old timbers found on Mount Ararat.

CHAPTER THREE

TREASURE SEEKERS

Over the centuries, treasure hunters of all kinds have risked and lost their lives in obsessive searches for the hidden riches of the past. From the desert tombs of the pharaohs to the dank, green forests of rural England to the ramshackle gold rush towns of the Wild West, they have sought the earth's legendary hoards.

At 1:55 A.M. on April 4, 1923, the Egyptian capital, Cairo, was plunged into darkness by a power failure. At precisely the same moment, in a Cairo hotel, an English aristocrat, Lord Carnarvon, died of pneumonia brought on by blood poisoning following a mosquito bite. Carnarvon had provided the financial backing for one of the most obsessive treasure hunts of all time, the search to uncover the tomb of the teenage pharaoh Tutankhamen in

Egypt's Valley of the Kings. And his death started the legend of the Curse of the Pharaohs.

With Carnarvon's support, British archeologist Howard Carter had sought the tomb for a quarter of a century, fighting against the mounting skepticism of his colleagues and almost impossible working conditions. Yet finally, on November 5, 1922, he was in a position to cable Carnarvon: "At last have made a wonderful discovery...." Tutankhamen's tomb had been found — the mummified body of the pharaoh surrounded by the numerous objects of gold and other precious metals with which he had been buried over 3,000 years before.

A dark legacy

Once the euphoria had died down, rumors began to circulate of a darker side to the pharaoh's legacy. Three weeks after the discovery, a sandstorm blew up around the entrance to the tomb. According to one account, a hawk, the royal emblem of the house of Egypt, emerged and swept majestically away from the mouth of the tomb toward the west, the traditional site of the "other world" beyond death in Egyptian mythology.

Guardian of the tomb

Was there a malevolent guardian of the tomb, left by the pharaohs more than 1,000 years before the birth of Christ? Could the ancients have used now-lost psychic talents to put curses on those who dared to defile their ancient burial sites or hoards of hidden royal treasures? Such apparently farfetched speculations were fed by one single detail of Carnarvon's death in Cairo six months after the opening of the tomb. The mosquito bite that had indirectly killed him was on his left cheek — and Tutankhamen's mummified body bore a scar in precisely the same place.

Over the following years, a seemingly unaccountably high number of deaths occurred among those connected with the project — from murders and suicides to car accidents and fatal illnesses. The

Anglo-Saxon armor
In 1939 the remains of a 1,000-year-old burial ship were discovered at Sutton Hoo, Suffolk, England. Fantastic jewelry was found, together with various domestic and military items, including this warrior's helmet.

one person to escape the supposed curse was Carter: he died of natural causes 17 years later, in 1939. Of course, skeptics have disputed that there was anything strange in the fate of Carnarvon or the other alleged victims of Tutankhamen's curse. But the belief that hidden treasures are defended by mystical forces is old and powerful.

Golden vessel
A Peruvian ceremonial water pot.

Myth and reality

In mythology stretching back to the beginning of civilization, secret hoards of treasure are depicted as being guarded by a monster or to be attained only after overcoming a series of challenges. In Nordic myths, for instance, the hoard of the Niebelungen was defended by a dragon that the hero must slay; and in the Greek legend of the Golden Fleece, Jason and the Argonauts could reach the precious goal of their quest only after many extraordinary adventures.

In the realm of treasure seeking, the border between myth and reality is always hard to draw. One of the greatest lost treasures of all time, for example, is that recorded in the story of El Dorado, which means "the gilded one." For a century after the discovery of America by Christopher Columbus in 1492, European adventurers sought the fabled gold in the as yet unexplored reaches of South America — and

Treasures of Ur
The royal treasures of the ancient Sumerian city of Ur were unearthed by Englishman Sir Leonard Woolley in the 1920's. This "He-Goat Caught in a Thicket" was found in the great death pit.

the search has continued into the 20th century. Yet many historians have claimed that El Dorado was never more than an illusion generated by the fever of greed. Even the adventurers who sought this fabulous wealth, many losing their lives in the hazardous quest, could not agree whether El Dorado was a city or a person! Yet there is now strong evidence that, behind the legend, there lay a solid basis in reality.

Golden inauguration

The version of the El Dorado story that now appears most credible concerned a priest-king so rich and powerful that he could afford to throw away vast quantities of gold and jewels.

This "gilded one" ruled on the shores of Lake Guatavita, a volcanic crater-lake some 30 miles north of what is now Bogotá in Colombia. The Spaniards learned that whenever a new king was appointed, he was dusted all over with pure gold and, accompanied by four chieftains, set off on a raft across the lake. On reaching the center of the lake, the king bathed in the waters, washing the gold dust off his body; at the same time a great pile of gold and emeralds would be tipped over the edge of the raft. This prodigious treasure presumably accumulated in the thick mud on the lake bottom.

The hunt for the gold began as early as 1545.

Ceremonial knife
Made in the 12th or 13th century A.D., this figure probably represents a Peruvian god. It is decorated with turquoises.

The Great Gold Buckle
Part of the Sutton Hoo treasure, this intricate buckle is made of over 14 ounces of solid gold.

The brother of one of the original Spanish conquistadors lowered the lake level by 10 feet, using a huge gang of slave laborers equipped with buckets. Some 5,000 pesos of gold were found, but the main body of the treasure eluded the searchers. Thirty-five years later a wealthy merchant from Bogotá, Don Antonio Sepulveda, obtained permission from the Spanish authorities to dredge the lake. A large Indian workforce cut a hole in the lake wall, causing the water level to drop by 15 feet. Gold objects and a huge emerald were found before the hole filled in.

Thwarted by nature

Over the next four centuries, there were many other efforts to locate the drowned hoard, yet all failed. At the beginning of the 20th century, a British company called Contractors Ltd. succeeded in entirely draining the lake by digging an underground tunnel. At first the bottom was so thick with mud that no one could walk on it, but by the following day, it had dried solid in the sun. Unfortunately by the time drilling equipment was brought in, the mud had blocked the tunnel, and the lake had filled up again.

In 1965, the Colombian government declared the lake a national monument, banning any further draining. Thus the prospect of discovering whether the story was myth or reality was lost.

Evidence turned up in 1969, however, that gave considerable credence to the entire story. In a cave near Bogotá, two peasants found a solid gold model of a raft, dating back to El Dorado's time, complete with the figures of the priest-king and his four chieftains. Perhaps all those who lost their lives in the quest for the elusive El Dorado had not been pursuing an illusion after all.

TREASURES LOST

Great finds, such as the Sutton Hoo burial ship, discovered in England in 1939, remind us of the lost treasures that are still waiting to be found.

Ark of the Covenant

Where, for example, are the great golden menorah, the Ark of the Covenant, and the Table of Shewbread that were carried off from Solomon's Temple in Jerusalem by the Roman emperor Titus in A.D. 70?

Crown jewels

Where are the crown jewels of King John of England? In the fall of 1216 the king's belongings, apparently including the royal regalia, were being transported across the treacherous tidal mud flats of the Wash between Norfolk and Lincolnshire. An unusually high tide washed over the team of porters, leaving no survivors, and no sign of the crown jewels.

Knights Templar

What has become of the treasure assembled over two centuries by the Knights Templar, the military order founded to protect pilgrims to the Holy Land? In 1307 the Templars' leaders were massacred and the order dispersed by King Philip IV of France. But they had time to conceal their riches, many of which must still lie hidden.

The golden raft of El Dorado?

SECRET HOARDS

"After terrifying brushes with a moray eel...Hamilton began to think that the treasure was guarded by some force he could not conquer."

THERE IS TREASURE HIDDEN all over the world, and every now and then somebody uncovers a new hoard. Sometimes it is found by accident, though not as often as many people would like to believe. Sometimes the story of missing treasure has been passed on from generation to generation, but its location has been forgotten. Many people have sought it, and at last, in what seemed the least likely place, it suddenly turns up. Sadly, human greed has not changed over the centuries, and tales of violence and death attach to many hidden hoards. These treasures seem to have a will-o'-the-wisp quality about them: they are found and lost, rediscovered, and then vanish again. And always, men are killed and lives are ruined. The treasure almost invariably seems cursed.

Treasure in the crypt

The story of the Tuamotu treasure is a case in point. It begins in Peru in 1859, when four mercenaries apparently learned of a great treasure stored in the crypt of the church at Pisco, on the coast of Peru. They were an unsavory bunch of rogues: a Spaniard, Diego Alvarez; an Englishman, Luke Barrett; an Irishman, Jack Killorain; and an American, Arthur Brown. It was a renegade priest, Father Matteo, who told them of the treasure: 14 tons of golden ingots, 7 great golden candlesticks encrusted with jewels, 38 diamond necklaces, 2 chests (one filled with uncut stones and the other with Spanish silver doubloons), and a great quantity of jeweled rings, bracelets, and crucifixes.

Alvarez and Killorain began to attend mass at the church at Pisco. When the time seemed right, they told the local priests that they had learned Father Matteo was planning to steal the treasure. Wouldn't it be a good idea, they said, to move it? The priests agreed and chartered a vessel, the *Bosun Bird*, to carry the treasure to another church up the coast at Callao. The mercenaries kindly offered their services as guards.

As soon as the ship was out at sea, they slaughtered the priests, the captain, and the crew, and set course westward in search of an uninhabited Pacific island. Eventually, in December 1859, they made a landfall in the Tuamotu Islands, part of French Oceania. There they found a small atoll that they believed was called Pinaki and, with a great deal of labor, sank most of the treasure in a small pool, keeping only a fraction of the

Pirate treasure
The popular image of the pirate burying his booty for safekeeping has little basis in reality — although this fact fails to deter treasure seekers in possession of "authentic" maps.

Commemorative coin
This coin was struck to commemorate William Phips's discovery of the Concepción *in 1687.*

SUNKEN TREASURE

On October 31, 1641, the merchant ship *Concepción*, a member of a Spanish treasure fleet, struck a coral reef north of what is now the Dominican Republic. Eleven days later the ship finally broke up and sank, taking its fabulous treasure to the bottom of the ocean. Only half of the 500 crew and passengers survived.

Locating the wreck

There were many attempts to find the wreck. Boston sea captain William Phips located the ship encased in coral 46 years later and brought up a substantial amount of treasure. But Phips had found only part of the wreck, and the many American, English, Spanish, and West Indian treasure seekers who tackled the problem over the centuries had no success at all.

Operation Phips

Then, in the 1970's, an archetypal treasure hunter, the American Burt D. Webber, decided that he would try to find the wreck. He named the expedition Operation Phips after his predecessor. An experienced diver, with a larger-than-life personality, Webber convinced hard-nosed investors to commit their dollars. His unfailing leadership and limitless energy inspired his long-suffering divers in their pursuit. The team's efforts were rewarded when, on November 30, 1978, the first of many coins was found. That day's entry in the log read: "Praise God, silver pieces of eight were recovered in great quantities." An immense treasure had been found — the hunter's perpetual dream realized.

Concepción's cargo
A diver with part of the haul.

gold for their immediate needs. They then sailed on to Australia where, off the coast near Cooktown, they scuttled the *Bosun Bird* and rowed ashore in a small boat, announcing themselves as shipwrecked mariners.

Lack of finance

Having covered their tracks successfully, they had planned to sail back and recover the bulk of the treasure. But the gold they had brought with them was insufficient to finance an expedition, and they could find no backers who would believe their cover story — that they had fortuitously stumbled upon a map of where the treasure was buried.

They decided to try to raise more money by working in the Australian gold fields. Soon afterwards, however, Alvarez and Barrett were killed, and Brown and Killorain, involved in a murder, were sentenced to 20 years' imprisonment. Brown died in prison.

In May 1912 a former gold prospector called Charles Howe showed some kindness to a tramp, a man he described as "altogether the most frightful-looking little dwarf that ever escaped out of a picture-book." Four months later, Howe was called to the deathbed of the tramp in a Sydney hospital. The man identified himself as "Japonica Jack" Killorain. He gave Howe a chart drawn by Alvarez and made him promise to search for the treasure. He died three hours later.

The pear-shaped pool

Howe sold all he possessed and arrived in Pinaki in February 1913, where he built himself a hut. For 13 long years he dug trenches in the sand of the beach without success, before he heard that another atoll was reputed to be the true site of the burial. This islet had all the essential landmarks: the coral pinnacle on the east side of the reef, the pear-shaped pool, and the seven blocks of coral close by.

Probing in the sand beside the pool with an iron bar, Howe struck wood and dug up a chest filled with uncut rubies, long diamond necklaces, and much more. After three more days, he

> ## Howe struck wood and dug up a chest filled with uncut rubies, long diamond necklaces, and much more.

discovered the chest of doubloons. But he had no way of transporting these finds; so he buried them again in sacks in the sand. Then he returned home to find backers for a proper expedition.

Six years later, in 1932, he had succeeded in organizing this expedition, but there were frustrating delays. To occupy the time, Howe decided to go prospecting in the Australian bush. Sadly, he was never heard of again.

Finally, in January 1934, the expedition — minus Charles Howe — arrived in Tahiti. There were six men, including the diver George Hamilton, who later wrote a book about the search. They found the atoll and dug where Howe had told them to, but found nothing. No doubt to protect his own interests, Howe had given them the wrong directions; so they turned next to the pear-shaped pool.

The floor of the pool was covered with sand and broken coral. Hamilton began searching the sand, and on his sixth attempt, six feet into the sand, his drill struck something that was neither sand nor rock. They built a wall of corrugated iron around the spot so that the sand could be excavated, but as fast as they dug the sand slid back from the

surrounding waters. After terrifying brushes with a giant octopus and the biggest moray eel he had ever seen, Hamilton began to think that the treasure was guarded by some force that he could not conquer.

Eventually the money ran out and the fateful expedition had to return to Australia. As far as anyone knows, there have been no further expeditions to the islands. The treasure is presumably still there, waiting to be discovered.

THE LOST DUTCHMAN MINE

Unfortunately, many stories of treasure have become so intertwined with legend, yarn spinning, and downright lies that the truth and the treasure, if it ever existed, appear to be gone forever. The Lost Dutchman Mine provides one such tale.

The mine is supposedly situated in the Superstition Mountains, 40 miles east of Phoenix. The first Europeans to see the mountains were probably Spaniards, who had traveled up from Mexico in the mid-16th century. They were told by the Indians that this was a sacred area, very rich in gold.

Presumably, Mexican miners heard the tales of untold riches, then disregarded the potential Indian threat in order to work the region. But the Apaches took their revenge when, in 1848, they massacred the miners.

Less than 20 years later, the "Dutchman" appeared on the scene. Jacob Waltz was in fact a German mining engineer who had apparently found the location of the Superstition Mountain mine. There were claims that a Mexican benefactor had provided him with a map. The tale may well have been a convenient cover story to explain away the sudden appearance of gold achieved by other, illegal, means.

Waltz and his accomplice, Jacob Weiser, did, however, travel into the mountains and return with gold. Unfortunately, their good

Manga Colorado
The Apache chief who led the 1848 massacre.

fortune came to an abrupt halt when they were attacked by Indians and Weiser was fatally wounded. Many others also perished in the search for the mine, often in sinister circumstances, but Waltz returned to the mountains over the years to collect further booty. Waltz died in 1891, leaving only sketchy, inadequate directions to the mine.

A 20th-century victim of the search for the mine was Adolph Ruth. An elderly American, Ruth disappeared into the mountains in 1931. Six months later his skull and then his body were found. He had been shot twice in the head and then decapitated. In his pocket investigators found a small book containing directions to the mine and the words *Veni, Vidi, Vici.* But neither the mine nor his murderer was found.

A further clue to the mine's whereabouts had been let slip by Weiser, who indicated that its position was marked by a large boulder. There was just such a boulder near the site of the old Indian massacre ground. In the late 1940's, engineer Alfred Strong Lewis was searching in the area when he decided to dislodge the "marker" boulder. Underneath it, he found a lode of rich ore, but it soon became obvious that this was not the main shaft. Perhaps that now lies awaiting discovery in the surrounding area.

Despite the fact that others have also lost their lives in the quest, treasure hunters still search the mountains with varying degrees of expertise, hoping to make their fortune.

Mountains of gold

Another hoard of Spanish gold is said to lie in the Hembrillo Basin west of the San Andres Mountains in New Mexico. The story begins near the end of the 18th century, when a French nobleman, Philippe La Rue, arrived in the area and discovered a gold mine. When the Spanish authorities in New Mexico heard the news, they sent out soldiers from Mexico City, who tortured La Rue to death in a vain attempt to make him divulge the location of the mine.

Many years later the Apache chief Victorio made his headquarters in the Hembrillo Basin, from which he led raids

> ## "Where gold goes, blood flows. Been a lotta blood flowed because of that hill, good buddy, and it's my guess it ain't done flowing yet. You'll see."
> ### Mrs. Ova Noss

along the Rio Grande Valley. He robbed mail coaches and churches, and it is said that he even carried off the treasure of the Emperor Maximilian of Mexico, who was deposed and shot in 1867. A small rocky hill, some 500 feet high, has been named Victorio Peak in memory of his profitable exploits.

Dramatic discovery

Seventy years later, in November 1937, a small hunting party, which included local homesteader Milton "Doc" Noss and his wife, Ova, set out from Hatch, New Mexico. Scrambling alone over the rocks of Victorio Peak, Noss stumbled onto a shaft that seemed to lead down into the very heart of the mountain. He sensibly kept the discovery to himself, and a few days later he and his wife returned to explore further with ropes and flashlights.

According to Noss, he soon discovered a cavern "big enough for a freight train," scattered with human skeletons. Noss counted 27 of them, each with hands bound behind its back. But he was even more struck by the

White Sands National Monument and Ova Noss

other contents of the cave — guns, swords, and saddles, a stack of leather pouches stuffed to the brims with gold, and "thousands of bars of gold, stacked like cordwood."

Rock fall

There is some evidence, in the form of photographs said to be in the possession of the Noss family, that "Doc" brought up a number of gold bars and other valuables during the next two years. But in 1939 he foolishly decided to make access to the treasure easier by blasting open the mouth of the cave. The result was a disastrous fall of tons of rock, which sealed up the opening.

It was not until February 15, 1946, that "Doc" Noss finally filed a claim on the Victorio Peak mine. In 1949 he went into

---

According to Noss, he discovered a cave, "big enough for a freight train," scattered with human skeletons.

---

partnership with a miner called Charles Ryan. They planned to tunnel the gold out of the cave and fly it across the Mexican border. The project was well advanced when Noss and Ryan quarreled violently, and Ryan shot Noss dead. By strange coincidence, on that very same day Noss's son, Marvin, whose part in the elaborate plan had been to pilot the plane carrying the treasure, was badly injured in an air crash.

Access denied

In 1953 the U.S. Army took over land west of the San Andres Mountains and turned it into the White Sands Missile Range.

Although Ova Noss pointed out that she had an entirely legitimate claim to mine on Victorio Peak, she was denied access. The zone was closed to everyone except officially authorized military personnel.

The White Sands affair has since developed into a long drawn-out legal battle. In 1963 the Denver Mint obtained

---

Those hundreds of gold bars, and even Emperor Maximilian's treasure, may yet be discovered.

---

permission to dig, between missile-testing schedules, from July 13 through September 17. Although thousands of tons of rock and earth were moved during the search, the entrance to the mine was not discovered.

Multiple claims

In 1972, nationally known attorney F. Lee Bailey announced that he represented 50 claimants who knew the location of the cave. Ova Noss was not among them. After lengthy legal action, in March 1977 the army allowed six claimants to mount a 14-day exploration on the missile range. Professional treasure hunter Norman Scott, head of Expeditions Unlimited Incorporated, was employed to make the attempt. Scott moved in an army of men equipped with an array of modern hardware from bulldozers to helicopters, but after 13 days' hard toil, the unsuccessful search of the mountains was finally abandoned.

The numerous gold seekers were denied access to the whole area for the next 12 years. But then, in 1989, the authorities permitted Norman Scott to explore Victorio Peak one more time. Those thousands of gold bars, and even the Emperor Maximilian's fabulous stolen treasure, may yet be discovered.

THE PRACTICAL SIDE

It seems obvious why so many expeditions in search of treasure have failed miserably. The adventurers have set off with large quantities of optimism, determination, and often greed, but generally with very little else. The sensible treasure hunter makes careful preparations.

Finding the facts

Rumors abound concerning the whereabouts of secret hoards. To avoid a haphazard approach, thorough research should be conducted into the background information. The location and history of the area should be studied, using reliable government survey maps.

Treasure trove

It is important to find out who would benefit from any valuable discovery. The regulations regarding the ownership of a treasure trove can be complicated and need thorough clarification before the actual search begins.

Choosing equipment

Equipment and clothing — and, if needed, weapons — should be chosen carefully, and expert advice sought where necessary.

The elements

In hot regions dehydration can be a killer. Exploration should be

undertaken only in winter, when temperatures are cooler and water is usually available.

Keeping track

Travel plans should be logged with family or friends. Diaries and maps should always be kept methodically.

QUEST FOR THE GRAIL

"I will make here a vow...I shall labour in the quest of the Grail...and never shall I return till I have seen it."
Sir Gawain in *Morte d'Arthur* by Sir Thomas Malory

Siege Perilous
In this painting by Scottish artist Sir William Russell Flint, Sir Galahad joins the knights of King Arthur's Round Table. Galahad alone is able to sit, unharmed, in the "Siege Perilous" — the Seat of Danger. This indicates that he is destined to find the Holy Grail.

THE FABULOUS AND MYSTERIOUS STORY of the Holy Grail first emerges obscurely from the mists of legend in the *Conte del Graal*, written about 1180 by the medieval French poet Chrétien de Troyes. This incredible tale, of which only a part has survived, tells of a Welsh youth, Perceval, living at the court of the English king Arthur.

Fearing that his mother is dying, Perceval sets off to journey homeward. He comes to a river where he meets a man fishing, who invites him to his nearby castle. In the castle Perceval encounters a squire carrying a white lance dripping with blood, and a beautiful girl bearing a Grail. The poet does not say exactly what the Grail is, but describes it as made of gold, set with jewels, and giving off a brilliant, unearthly light. At dinner, the Grail is passed in front of everyone as each course is served, but Perceval, the poem tells us, "did not ask concerning the Grail, whom one served with it."

Perceval is shown to his bed, and in the morning the castle is deserted. Riding away into the forest, he meets a maiden. She tells him that the castle belongs to the Fisher King, who has been crippled in battle by a javelin that has pierced both his thighs. Perceval should, she says, have asked about the lance and Grail, for his questions would have cured the Fisher King. Back at Arthur's court he is told that, if the Fisher King is not healed, "ladies will lose their husbands, lands will be laid waste...and many knights will die."

Origins of the Grail

This Grail of mystical powers became associated with the medieval Christian cult of the relics of the Crucifixion. The wood of the cross itself, the nails, the crown of thorns, the lance used by the centurion Longinus to pierce Christ's side,

▶ PAGE 96

QUEST FOR THE GRAIL

WHAT IS THE GRAIL?

The best-known image of the Grail is that of a gem-encrusted drinking cup made of a precious metal. It is supposedly the very cup used by Christ at the Last Supper, and then by Joseph of Arimathea to catch Christ's blood at the Crucifixion.

Kilkhampton cup
A 19th-century image of the cup used at the Last Supper.

Benevolent stone

In Wolfram von Eschenbach's 13th-century version of this story, *Parzival*, the Grail is a sacred stone, able to provide unlimited amounts of food and drink.

Holy bloodline

Some modern researchers believe that the Grail is not an object at all, but that it represents the bloodline of the family of Christ, the *Sangreal*, or royal blood.

Healing cauldron

Celtic legend says the Grail is a healing cauldron that is able to discriminate between good and evil. The deserving sick are placed in this cauldron to be cured.

Dramatic detail
The scenes on the inside of the Gundestrup bowl include one of a warrior being plunged into a large cauldron.

LONG AGO IN CAMELOT...

In the presence of King Arthur and the knights of the Round Table, the wizard Merlin predicts the birth of one who will sit in the "Siege Perilous" — the seat that is mortally dangerous to all but the knight who is to fulfill the task of finding the Grail.

LAUNCELOT, KING ARTHUR'S bravest knight, arrives in a pleasant town where the townspeople beg him to save a damsel who is being held captive in a tower by an enchantress. Launcelot frees the girl who is called Elaine, daughter of King Pelles. Together they ride to Pelles' kingdom. He is known as the Maimed King of the Wasteland Kingdom because, many years ago, a knight called Balin pierced his side with a spear. At this blow all the buildings in Pelles' kingdom tumbled to the ground, all vegetation withered, every fish left the waters, and Pelles' wound would not heal. Only the purest knight that ever lived could restore Pelles and his kingdom to life.

Elaine falls in love with Launcelot. Their union is encouraged by the king, who has prior knowledge that the result will be a son, Galahad, and that "by him the Holy Grail should be achieved." Launcelot is tricked into bed with Elaine, who uses sorcery to pretend to be his true love, King Arthur's wife, Queen Guinevere.

I Many years later the court is gathered in Camelot when a maiden arrives on horseback. She demands, on behalf of King Pelles, that Launcelot should travel with her to an abbey in the forest. There they find the fully grown Galahad, and Launcelot is asked to knight him. A few days later the new knight arrives in Camelot.

The knights are sitting at the Round Table when Galahad is led into the hall by an old man, who indicates that he should sit in the "Siege Perilous," the Seat of Danger. This he does and all the knights around realize that this is the "best knight of the world" who is destined to find the Holy Grail.

The Grail appears in Arthur's hall that very night. All present are struck dumb until the Grail has gone. Following the appearance of the Grail, the knights rise one after another and vow to go in search of it.

To the great sorrow of those who are left behind, 150 knights depart on the Grail quest. Some women wish to follow them but all of the knights swear that they will be celibate during the quest. At their going Arthur remembers Merlin's prophecy that the start of the Grail quest would signal the end of the glorious order of the knights of the Round Table.

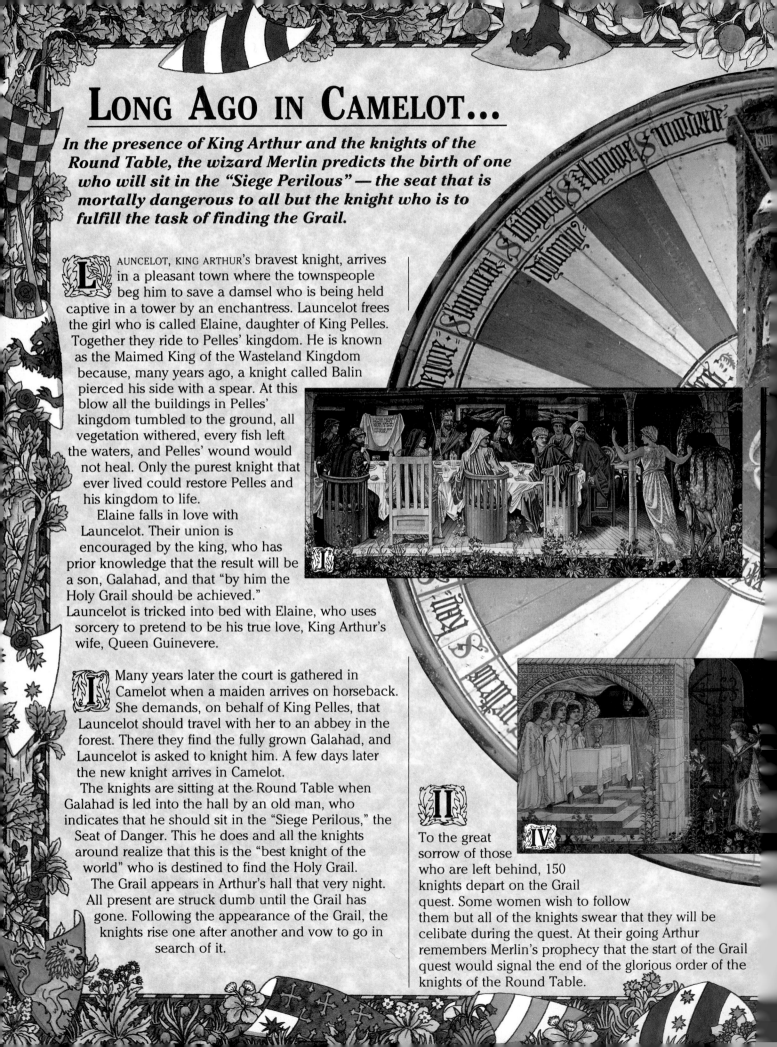

Last Supper and Joseph of Arimathea. As several of the knights fail in their quest, it is obvious that this is a result of the Grail sorting out the good from the sinners. During the knights' travels they have many further revelations made to them. Finally father and son, Launcelot and Galahad, are reunited. They spend six months sailing the seas, before they continue their quests alone, Launcelot being blown back out to sea and Galahad setting off into a forest.

Launcelot lands at the rear of a castle, which he enters. He comes to a locked room and, realizing that the Grail lies inside, he prays to be allowed to see it once more. The door opens and there, amidst dazzling light, is the Grail. Launcelot tries to enter the room but is transfixed. He falls into a coma and hovers between life and death for 24 days.

When Launcelot regains consciousness, he learns he is in the castle of King Pelles and that he will come no closer to finding the Grail, for his past sins hinder him and render him powerless. Launcelot realizes that his quest has ended and returns to Camelot.

Galahad, meanwhile, meets up with Bors and Percival, and they ride to King Pelles' castle. Galahad has finally returned home and he is greeted by King Pelles, who knows that the prophecy of the Grail is about to be realized.

IV In the presence of the Grail, the maimed King Pelles is brought before them. Christ himself appears from the Grail and feeds them with a marvelous sacrament, charging Galahad with the task of returning the Grail to the Holy Land and promising him the gift of spiritual life. Galahad uses the blood from a bleeding spear to cure King Pelles. The instant Pelles is healed his kingdom too comes back to life and as the three good knights ride away from his castle, they can smell the fresh perfume of newly budded flowers, leaves, and grasses and hear the sounds of birds singing.

Galahad, Percival, and Bors take the Grail back to the Holy Land, along with the spear. A year later Galahad is made king, but on his death shortly afterwards the vessel and the spear are taken up to Heaven by a Godly hand, along with his soul. Percival lives as a holy man until his death, just over a year later. Having buried Percival, Bors returns to Camelot to tell the remarkable tale of the Holy Grail.

Based on Sir Thomas Malory's Arthurian tale Morte d'Arthur, *written in about 1485.*

III On the first day the knights ride out as if in a single body, but on the second day they separate and ride in bands of two's and three's. The knights experience a series of adventures. Gradually the meaning of the quest becomes clear, as various hermits explain the origins of the Grail by telling the story of the

by Joseph of Arimathea, the man who, according to the Bible, buried Christ's crucified body. Joseph is supposed to have taken the Grail to Calvary and caught in it the blood that flowed from the wound in Christ's side. But it was the Burgundian poet Robert de Borron, writing in about 1200, who identified the Grail of Joseph with the cup used at the Last Supper, when Christ said "This is my blood of the covenant, which is poured out for many." Matthew 26:28

A few years later the Bavarian poet Wolfram von Eschenbach wrote another version of Perceval's adventures,

> ## "The Grail was the fruit of blessedness...its delights were very like what we are told of the Kingdom of Heaven."

Parzival, in which the Holy Grail is a stone guarded by a secret order of knights named Templeisen. Parzival comes to the hall of the Maimed King, and sees the Grail, "which surpasses all earthly perfection." At dinner, "whatsoever one reached his hand for, he found it ready, in front of the Grail, food warm or food cold, dishes new or old, meat tame or game...for the Grail was the fruit of blessedness, such abundance of the sweetness of the world that its delights were very like what we are told of the Kingdom of Heaven."

The story of the Holy Grail was never supported by the Christian church. And yet, as the Grail stories proliferated, they became ever more Christian. Authors wrote about the Grail in a religious context, and stressed that only the pure could hope to see it. In the 13th-century *Queste del Saint Graal*, the saintly Sir Galahad

Seal of the knights
This Templar seal shows two knights riding one horse, and bears the inscription "Seal of the Soldiers of Christ." The Knights Templar have often been identified with the Templeisen guardians of the Grail in Wolfram von Eschenbach's Parzival. *Much speculation surrounds the whereabouts of the Templars' great fortune which was lost in the 14th century. There are also those who claim that the knights knew of the secret location of the Grail itself.*

the shroud in which His body was wrapped — all these were eagerly sought after, and fragments of extremely doubtful origin were lovingly revered. But there was another priceless relic that everybody searched for fruitlessly: the cup used by Christ at the Last Supper. In time this came to be identified as the Holy Grail.

Within 20 years of Chrétien de Troyes's Grail story, the tale had been elaborated upon by writers all over Europe, and it has remained the subject of commentary and controversy ever since. The many versions of the Grail legend differ in significant ways, but all contain enough similarities to link them in some way.

In a second tale, written shortly after de Troyes's death, the knight Sir Gawain sees the Grail, which moves about the dinner table by itself, filling the wine cups and serving each course. The white lance dripping with blood, he is told, is that used by the centurion Longinus to pierce Christ's side. Another author explains that the Grail was made

Knights Templar
A 13th-century effigy of a member of the military religious order.

seeks and eventually finds the Grail. But he is dying, and at his death: "...the two remaining companions saw quite plainly a hand come down from Heaven, but not the body it belonged to. It proceeded straight to the Holy Vessel and took both it and the lance, and carried them up to Heaven, to the end that no man since has ever dared to say he saw the Holy Grail."

Magical objects

Over the centuries and throughout the world storytellers and scribes have found a rapt audience for their tales of a magical object, its origins shrouded in mystery, that will one day be found and

Joseph of Arimathea
Could this enigmatic biblical character really have traveled from the Holy Land to England, bringing the Holy Grail with him?

reveal its secret powers. Elements of the Grail story appear in many pre-Christian myths. The Celtic gods known as the Tuatha de Danaan possessed a magic cauldron, an all-conquering spear, a sword that could not be overcome, and the Lia Fail, the stone of fate. Similar objects occur in legends in Egypt and China. Perhaps humankind simply revels in inventing mysteries for which there are no easy answers.

Glimmer of truth

But could there be a reality behind the proliferation of Grail myths? Some people have certainly believed so, and have attempted to locate the story in the real history of Britain. The quest for the Grail became an essential part of the story of King Arthur, and gradually the sacred relic became associated with Glastonbury in Somerset, supposedly Arthur's "sweet isle of Avalon," where he ruled over his British kingdom. It was said that Joseph of Arimathea had carried the Grail across Europe until he reached Glastonbury, where he founded

> **Perhaps humankind simply revels in inventing mysteries for which there are no easy answers.**

the first Christian church in England. His staff, stuck into the earth, grew into the Glastonbury thorn tree, which flowered every Christmas Day. And the Grail was hidden in the Chalice Well, which for centuries was renowned for its miraculous healing waters.

Joseph was said to have been accompanied by his brother-in-law, Bron, a name that is also given to the Fisher King in more than one of the Grail romances. This is sufficiently close to that of Bran, the hero of a Celtic version

The Gundestrup cauldron

CELTIC CONNECTIONS
The Grail story has much in common with Celtic legends from the pre-Christian era.

The Phantom's Frenzy
In the Irish story *The Phantom's Frenzy*, the hero, Conn of the Hundred Battles, visits the hall of the sun god Lug. He is served by a girl in a golden crown, who before giving him ale asks, "To whom shall this cup be given?" Lug replies, "Serve it to Conn of the Hundred Battles."

The thirteen treasures
In the *Mabinogion*, a collection of Welsh stories, four magic vessels must be found for a wedding feast: a cup, which provides the finest drink; a platter on which all can find the meat they desire; a never-empty drinking horn; and the cauldron of Dyrnawg. This cauldron is also listed in the 16th-century *Thirteen Treasures of the Island of Britain*. It would only boil meat for a brave man.

Restoring life
The cauldron that belonged to Bran the Blessed, also in the *Mabinogion*, would restore the dead to life: "A man of thine slain today, cast him into the cauldron, and by tomorrow he will be as well as he was at the best...."

A cauldron, or bowl, that adds substance to the tale was found in a peat bog at Gundestrup in northern Denmark. Scenes on the inside include a warrior being plunged into a large receptacle.

HITLER AND THE LANCE

Like the legendary Holy Grail, the spear of Longinus is said to date from the time of the Crucifixion and is traditionally believed to hold the key to untold powers. To many notorious leaders throughout history its possession has always been highly coveted, down to the Third Reich of Adolf Hitler.

"BUT WHEN THEY came to Jesus, and saw that he was already dead, they did not break his legs. But one of the soldiers pierced his side with a spear, and at once there came out blood and water." John 19:33 – 34

Thus the centurion Longinus fulfilled the prophecy that not a bone of Christ's body would be broken at His death. The spear was inevitably sought as an invaluable relic by medieval Christians.

Over the centuries there have been several possible claimants to the title Sacred Lance, but it is the spear to be found in the old palace of the Habsburg emperors — the Hofburg in Vienna — that holds the most authentic claim to the name. According to Germanic tradition, in the ninth century the lance was carried by the first Holy Roman emperor, Charlemagne, through 47 victorious campaigns. Charlemagne met his death only when he accidentally dropped the lance. The tales of the spear's magical powers grew as it passed through the hands of Saxon and Hohenstauffen rulers. It was possessed for a while by Frederick Barbarossa, son of the Hohenstauffen dynasty, Holy Roman emperor, and conqueror of Italy. Barbarossa met the same fate as Charlemagne: he dropped the lance as he crossed a stream and died just minutes later. The spear eventually passed to the Habsburgs.

Adolf Hitler

Adolf Hitler, a penniless painter of watercolors in Vienna in 1913, was fascinated by the lance and the stories that linked it with generations of conquering German emperors. On March 14, 1938, as chancellor of Germany, he proclaimed the annexation of Austria into the Third Reich, and within days had given orders for

The Crucifixion
In this painting by 15th-century Flemish artist Hans Memling, the lance of the Roman centurion Longinus is shown piercing Christ's side.

the Habsburg regalia to be carried off to Nuremberg, the birthplace of the Nazi movement. It was as if he believed that possession of the lance would make him as powerful a conqueror in Europe as its former owners.

On October 13 the lance was loaded onto an armored train and, accompanied by an armed S.S. guard, was taken to St. Catherine's Church in Nuremberg. For more than five years Hitler held undisputed sway in Europe; then came D-Day and the Allied landings. After heavy bombing of Nuremberg in October 1944, the lance and the rest of the Habsburg regalia were hurriedly buried in a specially constructed vault.

Six months later, the American Seventh Army surrounded the city and, after four days of formidable bombardment, eventually took possession. On April 30, 1945, the lance was discovered in its underground chamber and seized in the name of the U.S. government. It is thought that it was on that same evening, a few hundred miles away, in his bunker in Berlin, that Hitler put a pistol to his head and shot himself.

Object of power
The spear is part of The Habsburg treasure, now to be found in Vienna. German dictator Adolf Hitler allegedly became obsessed with the lance and believed that, if it was in his possession, its power would enable him to achieve his ambitions to conquer Europe and beyond. Hitler may have thought that the mystical qualities of the lance had assisted the many conquering German emperors who preceded him.

King Arthur
The story of King Arthur is ever popular. So that no knight might appear superior to the others, they sat around a democratic Round Table. It was the quest for the Holy Grail that caused the knights to depart from Camelot, leaving their king to mourn the end of the "truest knighthood that ever were seen together."

of the story, to suggest that there is a connection. And above the waters of the River Dee at Llangollen, which Perceval would have had to cross on his way back into Wales, stand the ruins of Dinas Bran, Bran's castle. Is this, then, the home of the mysterious Fisher King?

There are other claimants. The Templeisen, who guarded the Grail in Wolfram von Eschenbach's *Parzival*, have been identified with the Knights Templar, a warrior order founded in 1118. The order was dispersed, and many of the knights executed, early in the 14th century, but much of their wealth was never recovered. During the last 200 years, many people have claimed to be the inheritors of the

Templar tradition and to know their secrets, and some have even said that they knew the whereabouts of the Holy Grail itself. But without some solid evidence these are empty claims. Recently, in France, it has been suggested that the word *Sangreal* (as the Holy Grail appears in some early manuscripts) should be read as *sang real* (royal blood) and that the reference is to the descendants of the Frankish Merovingian kings, whose line died out in A.D. 752, or even to those of the blood of the family of Christ.

Today, in the museum in Glastonbury, there is a bronze bowl, neatly decorated with a circle of studs. Could this really be the Holy Grail?

In 1190, just as the first tale of the Grail was being written, the monks of Glastonbury claimed to have found the grave of Arthur, but the bones they excavated have long been lost. Today, in the museum in the town, there is a bronze bowl, small but beautifully made, and neatly decorated with a circle of studs. It is clearly a ceremonial object, not a domestic one, and is believed to have been used in rituals by the lake dwellers who had their settlement nearby. Could this really be the Holy Grail? It remains overwhelmingly probable that the sacred chalice is only an object of myth.

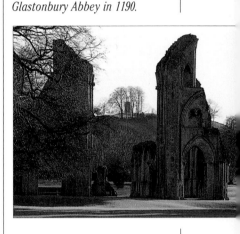

The ruins of the abbey
The mortal remains of King Arthur and Queen Guinevere were said to have been found in the ancient cemetery of Glastonbury Abbey in 1190.

The sacred chalice?
This unassuming bowl, dating from 250 B.C., fits the popular image of the Grail and can be found in the museum at Glastonbury.

CHAPTER FOUR

BREAKING THE RULES

It appears that there may be living among us certain individuals not bound by the physical and mental rules of life — individuals like the medium D. D. Home, who was apparently capable of enduring extreme heat with no effect, of practicing levitation, and even of changing the shape and size of his own body.

No medium was more intrigued by his own paranormal powers than the extraordinary Scottish-American psychic D. D. Home, and few have been as willing to submit to scientific investigation.

Daniel Dunglas Home was born in Scotland in 1833 and grew up in Hartford, Connecticut. It was in the United States that he began to develop his psychic powers and came to rival the originators of

DISAPPEARING ACT

At one time or another most people have wished they could disappear. During the 1960's, Dr. William Neff apparently became suddenly invisible on three occasions, demonstrating a talent that would have helped his career as a stage magician no end. But he had no control over its onset and was not even aware that it was occurring when it did.

Once he vanished during his act in Chicago, and another time before his terrified wife at home.

Dr. William Neff

Expert witness

The third occasion was witnessed by the broadcaster Long John Knebel, who was himself highly skeptical about paranormal phenomena. Knebel described what happened in his book *The Way Out World*. He was watching Neff perform at the Paramount Theatre in New York City, when "it seemed that Neff's body was becoming minutely translucent" until "you could see the traveler curtain clearly behind his transparent figure."

Even as he faded from view, Neff's voice remained perfectly audible. Then, wrote Knebel: "Gradually a rather faint outline, like a very faint pencil sketch of Neff, appeared again." Neff himself claimed to have been completely unaware of the event.

Daniel Dunglas Home

the spiritualist movement, the Fox sisters, in popularity. He went to London in 1855 and soon attracted the attention of the city's fashionable society.

Overnight sensation

Home could perform an enormous repertoire of improbable feats. As well as the raps and spirit messages common to every séance then and now, he could cause heavy Victorian tables and chairs to rise into the air — and, on occasion, the people sitting in the chairs as well. He often materialized disembodied hands that then floated about the séance room, moving objects and writing messages — these hands could be grasped, but then melted away on human contact. Musical instruments would float and play at Home's command. Trumpets and accordions were favorites, and were often brought by skeptics who suspected that Home's own instruments were mechanically operated. His extraordinary physical feats included plunging his face and hair into hot coals, bodily levitations, and spectacular stretchings. Witnesses to these elongations claimed to see his flesh distorting as he grew up to 12 inches taller.

Unlike most mediums of the era, Home did not hold his séances in darkness. He operated in subdued light — gaslight turned down low or the light from a large

Victorian fireplace — otherwise some of his effects, such as floating lights, would have been scarcely visible. But the light was certainly clear enough for his every action to be seen. He had no assistant, as other mediums often did. On innumerable occasions he performed at short notice in houses he had never previously visited, which offered him no chance to set up any secret apparatus in

---

Witnesses claimed to see Home's flesh stretching and distorting as he grew up to 12 inches taller.

---

advance. And he was always willing to be searched before a sitting. It is not surprising that several stage magicians who attended Home's sessions, in the hope of proving him a fraud, confessed themselves completely unable to explain what they had seen. In his book *Lights and Shadows of Spiritualism,* published in 1877, Home himself spent many pages castigating fake mediums and the tricks they used to gull the credulous.

Legendary levitation

The authenticity of many of Home's own feats are not beyond question — in particular, doubts surround his most famous act of levitation. The legend says that on the night of either December 13 or 16, 1868, in front of three suitably astonished witnesses — Capt. Charles Wynne, Lord Adare (later the earl of Dunraven), and the Master of Lindsay (later Lord Lindsay) — Home actually floated out of one fourth-story window of a London house and then came back in through another.

But exactly what did happen on that memorable night has never been satisfactorily determined.

Not only is the precise date of the whole event in question, but the witnesses failed to agree on which London house they were actually in that night, on the weather conditions, on the size and number of windows, or even on which floor the levitation took place. Capt. Wynne's only recorded comment on the event was perhaps the most reliable: "Home went out of one window and came in at another."

Defying gravity and belief

Almost the only thing Lindsay and Adare agreed on was that Home exited from a window in the room next to the one in which they were sitting. He did not float out of the window before their eyes. He left the room, telling them on no account to move from their places, and then reappeared standing upright outside the window of the room he had just left. He opened the window and climbed in, presumably from the balcony. Was it levitation that transported Home across empty space that night? Or, more mundanely, was he able physically to climb from window to window to fake the effect?

Whatever the answer, Home was never caught cheating in any of his demonstrations, which numbered over

---

> ## "I was thinking how astonished a policeman would have been if he had looked up and seen me floating between the windows."
> **D. D. Home**

1,500 in the course of 25 years. He impressed the French emperor Napoleon III and the Russian czar Alexander II with his powers, and was happy to be investigated by some of the most eminent scientists of the day. Witnesses overwhelmingly agreed that he remained fully visible during séances and several feet away from where the

most bizarre phenomena were seen to occur. His accordion, which so often played by itself, is now in the possession of the Society for Psychical Research in London. It contains no clockwork or other non-musical mechanism, nor any indication that it has ever done so. Perhaps most significant in any assessment of Home's abilities, he never took money for his demonstrations. If he was a fraud, he was one of the greatest frauds ever. If he was genuine, he was one of the most extraordinary and inexplicable of men.

THE FOX SISTERS

During the second half of the 19th century, the middle and upper classes in the United States, Britain, and much of Europe became fascinated, if not indeed obsessed, by séances and mediums. Yet the spiritualist movement had started modestly enough, when two young girls, the Fox sisters, suddenly claimed to possess a highly unusual talent – the ability to communicate with the dead. Genuine or not, the girls were certainly in possession of some extraordinary talents.

Margaretta Fox

The world first heard of the power of paranormal communication as a direct result of the strange events that occurred in a simple wooden house in Hydesville, New York, on March 31, 1848. For some time before, the inhabitants, Margaret and John Fox and their two daughters Catherine, aged 12, and Margaretta, aged 14, had been disturbed at all times of the day and night by inexplicable rattlings of the walls and various items of furniture.

Pioneering spirits

According to a sworn statement signed by Mrs. Fox: "The children heard the rapping and tried to make similar sounds by snapping their fingers. Cathie clapped her hands and said 'Mr Splitfoot, do as I do!' The sound instantly followed with the same number of raps."

Before long, the girls had established an alphabetical code to interrogate the noisy entity. They soon became convinced that the noises were being made by the spirit of a 31-year-old peddler who had been

Cathie Fox

murdered and whose remains lay buried under the house.

Within just a few short days, the sisters, and the mysterious raps, were a local sensation. Two years later the girls had become national celebrities, performing a full repertoire that included table-turning and "direct voices," in which the spirits spoke directly through them. It was not long before many others found that they, too, possessed the psychic gift that enabled them to produce these extraordinary manifestations, and parlor séances soon became all the rage.

Fall from grace

The Fox sisters continued to work as mediums during the 1850's, while spiritualism spread throughout the Western world. Then, in 1857, Margaretta's husband, the Arctic explorer Elisha Kent Kane, died. Without his support, she took to drink and drugs. The pressures of celebrity so young also took their toll on Catherine; she too became an alcoholic. In 1888, in desperate need of money, the two sisters were paid $1,500 by the *New York Herald* to confess to fraud and deceit. A year later, they retracted the confessions.

Did they cheat? They were never detected doing so. And in 1904, after their deaths, a wall in the house in Hydesville collapsed, revealing the remains of a body, whose identity was never discovered. This indicated that something quite real may have lain behind the birth of spiritualism and the remarkable, and influential, careers of Margaretta and Cathie Fox.

BODY MAGIC

The human body is sometimes capable of the most amazing feats — wild talents in apparent defiance of the laws of nature.

Hindu ritual
Thaipusam festival, Singapore.

HOW CAN SOME PEOPLE walk on burning coals, withstand injuries that should cause unbearable pain, or apparently float in the air? Such abilities have often been dismissed as trickery, or else attributed to some supernatural agency.

In recent years, medical research has proven that human beings can change their body's functioning through the power of the mind. This line of investigation could hold the key to many, if not all, apparently inexplicable physical abilities.

Still, no one knows exactly how this power of the mind could actually work, or why faith plays such a large part in these feats.

THE POWER OF THE LORD

Strange physical feats have often been attributed to the power of God. It is a Christian tradition that those blessed with great godliness can also be given strange physical powers. According to Catholic histories of the lives of the saints:

◆ St. Francis of Paola (died 1507) could handle fire without ever being burned.

◆ During religious ecstasies and devout prayers St. Catherine de Ricci (1522–90) was known to give off sweet odors.

◆ Other saints have been given the gift of bodily elongation in which parts of the body are stretched, causing excruciating pain. On one occasion, St. Catherine of Genoa's (1447–1510) arm is said to have grown by more than five inches.

◆ In 1497, 21 distinguished witnesses saw Blessed Stefana Quinzani suffer painful bodily changes in imitation of Christ's suffering on Calvary.

◆ St. Teresa of Ávila (1515–1582) often levitated during her ecstatic prayers. "It seemed to me," she wrote, "as if a great force beneath my feet lifted me up. I confess that it threw me into great fear."

Religious offering
A young dervish in Iran pierces his cheek, apparently without pain.

Suffer the faithful

Religious faith seems to enable some believers to do the impossible. They are protected from the heat of fire, the sting of venomous snakes, and the pain of self-mutilation by their unquestioning belief in their gods.

Devotees of some Hindu cults, and the dervish sect of Islam, prepare themselves by fasting and praying before sticking skewers and hooks into their flesh or walking on fire. The true believer seems to come through the experience remarkably unscathed; others, perhaps lacking in true faith, have been known to suffer grievous injuries.

A halo of spikes
The wounds do not bleed and leave no scars.

Eating glass
Attich Abdellah from Morocco.

Monsieur Mangetout
Michel Lotito and his potentially lethal diet.

Human pincushions

Religious devotees engaged in ritual self-mutilation appear to feel no pain, even when hanging in mid-air with hooks in their backs. Scientists suspect that they may be able to produce large quantities of endorphins, the morphinelike substances that are manufactured by the brain to block pain.

This does not explain, however, why the wounds neither bleed nor leave scars. Perhaps the explanation lies in the superb control many Eastern mystics have over their circulatory systems — it is known that they can slow their heart beat and change their blood pressure; it may be that they can also reduce the blood flow to their capillaries.

Fire-eating

To spit fire, fire-eaters fill their mouths with a flammable liquid and blow it out at a fire stick. To swallow fire, they put a burning stick in the mouth; then they quickly close their lips around it. The fire is thus deprived of oxygen and cannot burn. When the stick is removed, it will catch fire again, giving the illusion that it had been burning all the time. No amateur should attempt these tricks, for even professionals have suffered hideous injuries.

Strange eating habits

Eating metal, glass, and other indigestible items has long been a favorite of sideshow performers, the most famous of whom is the Frenchman Michel Lotito, known as Monsieur Mangetout (Mr. Eat-All). He travels the world providing weird entertainment with his outrageous dietary habits. He says that he eats an average of two pounds of metal a day, washed down with mineral oil and gallons of water. Over the years he has eaten bicycles, television sets, and even a Cessna 150 light aircraft (which took over two years of dedicated munching).

There does seem to be a rational explanation for Lotito's abilities. Scientists have found that his stomach and intestinal walls are twice as thick as the average person's, while his digestive juices are unusually strong. Lotito himself ascribes his success to the time and date of his birth — midday on June 15, 1950 — which he believes holds some unspecified mystical significance, as it is exactly halfway through the century.

Hung from hooks

A Hindu anticipates his painful religious ordeal.

Playing with fire
French fire-eaters demonstrate their dangerous skills to the Parisian public.

Secrets of the Sadhus

The Sadhus, or holy men of India, spend a lifetime searching for ultimate union with God. Along the way, they master the eight great siddhis (accomplishments), among them levitation, telepathy, clairvoyance, premonition and, finally, nirvana. Through meditation, they are able to produce physical changes in their body temperature, heart rate, blood pressure, and brain waves that enables them to withstand pain and cold and to remain immobile and unblinking for long periods of time.

Mind control
A fire-walking experiment, Granada Hills, California, 1984.

Sparks fly
A spectacular Balinese fire dance.

Fire-walking

Fear of fire's searing heat is universal, and yet across the world, from Bali to Mexico, there are people who are able to overcome that fear and walk triumphantly across beds of burning coals unscathed. In fact, fire-walking has become popular even in the United States in recent years. Many fire-walkers feel that they are protected by their gods. Scientists have suggested a number of more mundane theories – the "leidenfrost" effect in which sweat forms an insulating cushion of steam under the feet; the walker's minimal contact with the ground (lasting less than half a second per step); the trancelike state of most fire-walkers, which produces an anesthetic effect; or even the fact that burning embers are poor conductors of heat so the fire is just not very hot. But what none of these theories can explain is why clothes do not burn or why, if fire-walking is governed by ordinary physical laws, some fire-walkers are seriously injured, while others seem to escape completely unscathed.

Psychic entertainer
English magician Doc Shiels levitates his daughter.

Lift-off
American levitator Peter Sugleris leaves the ground.

Walking on air

Levitation, the ability to suspend the laws of gravity that bind us to the earth, is generally considered to be impossible. But these photographs of Doc Shiels and Peter Sugleris seem to suggest otherwise. And with little thought of magic or mysticism, school-children all over the world play levitation games in which a group of youngsters try to lift a friend using only their fingers. Indian holy men also claim to be able to levitate by using their mystical powers, but there has never been a scientific study to prove it.

Scientific application

Yogis are reflective and mystical devotees of the Hindu philosophy that believes in the suppression of the activities of the mind, body, and will, with the ultimate aim of freeing the inner self. They have been able to provide valuable clues for researchers about the power of the mind over the body. Scientists believe that yogis are able to produce "theta" brain waves (slow brain waves common to the dreaming stages of sleep) through meditation, and to slow their breathing and heartbeat at will.

Contemplative stance

A holy man meditates while standing on one leg at Varanasi, India.

Rope trickery

The Indian rope trick, in which a magician makes a rope rise into the air, becoming stable enough to support the weight of a child assistant who climbs it, has fascinated experts and audiences for years. There are explanations as to how the trick is carried out, such as suspending a wire 30 feet above ground between two hills, surreptitiously attaching a hook to the rope, and then throwing the hook over the wire. The almost impossible requirements, both of location and skill, may explain why the trick is so rarely performed — thus ensuring its cult status.

Daubed with ash

A holy man assumes the classic meditative pose.

Science meets mysticism

A yogi is prepared for a biofeedback test.

The Indian rope trick

The trick as performed in the mid-1930's by Karachi and Kyder — eccentric Englishman Arthur Darby and his son.

MIND OVER MATTER

For thousands of years, mystics and yogis from cultures all over the world have been able to regulate their own physical state through the act of meditation. Now similar powers are being used in the most advanced hospitals in the Western world.

Biofeedback therapy

Electrodes measure the patient's pulse rate, and the variations are represented visually by changes in the brightness of an image.

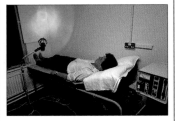

Conscious control

In the medical profession, some 20 or 30 years ago, the pioneers of biofeedback technique concluded that the only reason we could not control our so-called involuntary functions, such as heartbeat and blood pressure, was because we could not actually see or hear them. It followed that if we could be made conscious of what is happening inside our bodies, we would then be able to exercise some control over those areas.

Vital functions

Electronic instruments have since been developed that can literally — and quite painlessly — "feed back," both visually and audibly, information about automatic internal functions. Patients are trained to respond to this information. Thus in witnessing a visual display of, for example, their own heartbeat, they are able to concentrate on it and regulate it. So, although no one knows exactly how it works, biofeedback has demonstrated the power of the mind over bodily functions.

THE IMMORTAL COUNT

"This extraordinary man...would say in an easy, assured manner that he was 300 years old, that he knew the secret of the Universal Medicine, that he possessed a mastery over nature, that he could melt diamonds...all this, he said, was a mere trifle to him."
Giacomo Girolamo Casanova

ON THE TRAIL OF THE COUNT
Over the centuries there have been many sightings of Count de Saint-Germain, and many theories as to his origins and his ultimate, unconfirmed, demise.

◆ **1600's Transylvania** Born illegitimate son of Prince Franz-Leopold Ragoczy.

◆ **1600's Bohemia** Born illegitimately in Lentmeritz, to a noble Rosicrucian.

◆ **1710 Italy** Born in San Germano, son of a tax collector.

◆ **1710 Italy** Seen, appearing to be a 45-year-old man, in Venice, by Countess von Georgy.

◆ **1737 Persia** Five years at the court of the shah.

◆ **1760 France** At the house of Madame de Pompadour in Paris, seen again by Countess von Georgy still looking 45 years old.

◆ **1784 Germany** His death reported in Eckernförde.

◆ **1785 Germany** Seen with pioneer hypnotist Anton Mesmer.

◆ **1793 France** Present at Marie Antoinette's execution in Paris.

◆ **1799 France** Witness to Napoleon's seizure of power.

◆ **1804, 1813, 1820 France** Seen by Countess d'Adhémar.

◆ **1897 France** Singer Emma Calve autographs her picture to Saint-Germain — "the great chiromancer, who has told me many truths."

◆ **1972 France** On television, Richard Chanfray claims to be the mysterious count.

IN 1760, WHEN COUNTESS VON GEORGY heard a footman announce the arrival of Count de Saint-Germain at a soiree at the Paris house of Madame de Pompadour, mistress to the French king Louis XV, the aging aristocratic lady was intrigued. She had known a Count de Saint-Germain in 1710, in Venice, where her husband had been a diplomat.

Perhaps, the countess asked, this was the present count's father?

"No, Madame," he answered, "but I myself was living in Venice at the end of the last and the beginning of this century; I had the honor to pay you court then."

"Forgive me, but that is impossible!" exclaimed the startled countess. "The Count de Saint-Germain I knew in those days was at least 45 years old. And you, at the outside, are that age at present."

"Madame," replied Saint-Germain with a smile, "I am very old."

"But then you must be nearly 100 years old," said the countess in amazement.

"That is not impossible," answered the count. And he proceeded to give the countess such a detailed account of life in Venice 50 years earlier that she could only accept that he was telling the truth.

Biblical connections
Saint-Germain was to be connected with even more startling statements than this. It was said that he had been a guest at the wedding at Cana when Jesus of Nazareth performed his first miracle, turning the water into wine. Apparently one of his friends in those days had been Anne, the Virgin Mary's mother, and he himself had proposed that she should be recognized as a saint — in A.D. 325, at the Council of Nicaea.

Such claims are fantastic, but even the verifiable facts about Saint-Germain are extraordinary. He first came to the notice of European high society in Vienna in 1742, where he arrived after five years at the shah of Persia's court. There he had learned the jeweler's craft, and to speak the native language, Farsi; he also spoke fluent French, German, Dutch, Spanish, Portuguese, Russian, and English, and knew Chinese, Sanskrit, ancient Greek, Latin, and Arabic as well.

Vital symbols
For the alchemist, the sun and the moon represent the path through life, as well as rebirth and possible immortality.

Modern count
In 1972 Richard Chanfray claimed to be Saint-Germain, still alive in the 20th century. Chanfray later committed suicide.

Over the next four decades Saint-Germain was constantly on the move, staying in the major towns of Europe for brief periods and dazzling everyone he met with his prowess on the violin, his diamond-studded clothes, his ability as a painter (he had perfected a remarkable technique for painting jewels), his brilliant conversation, and his unchanging youthfulness. In the mid-1740's he carried out secret diplomatic missions on behalf of King Louis XV in England, and then did the same at the Hague in 1760, where he met up with another adventurer on a diplomatic mission, the infamous lover Casanova.

In 1768 he went to the court of Catherine the Great in Russia, where for two years he advised the commander of the imperial Russian armies in a war against Turkey. With the Turks defeated, he left Russia and traveled to Germany. In 1779 in Hamburg he met Prince Charles of Hesse-Cassel, and went to live in the Prince's castle at Eckernförde for the next five years; and it is there that, according to the parish records, he died on February 27, 1784.

Life after death?
According to many others, however, the count did not die in Eckernförde. A year after his reported death, Saint-Germain was seen in Wilhelmsbad in Germany with the pioneer hypnotist Anton Mesmer. In 1788 he was seen in Venice and Vienna, and in Paris where, still looking no older than 45, Saint-Germain visited the Countess d'Adhémar, an intimate friend of Queen Marie Antoinette, to warn the French royal family of the coming revolution; both women recorded the event in their diaries. Countess d'Adhémar reported seeing him, still looking like a man in his mid-forties, five more times: in 1793, when Marie Antoinette was guillotined; in 1799, when Napoleon seized power in France; and in 1804, 1813, and 1820. Although the existence of the countess

and her diaries has often been questioned, according to Mrs. Cooper-Oakley, author of a comprehensive volume on the life of the count published in 1912, there are documents pertaining to Saint-Germain in the possession of the d'Adhémar family.

The saga continues
And still the mysterious count's reappearances continued. In 1897 an autographed portrait of the French singer Emma Calve was dedicated to Saint-Germain, and in Paris in the 1970's a man called Richard Chanfray claimed to be the still-living count.

So exactly who was — or is — the Count de Saint-Germain? Some of the wilder stories about him — such as those

---

Voltaire described Saint-Germain as "a man who never dies, and who knows everything."

---

linking him with the Holy Family — were almost certainly rumors spread by Saint-Germain's enemies at the French court to make him appear ridiculous.

But even the 18th-century French philosopher Voltaire, habitually a rational and skeptical observer of the world around him, described Saint-Germain as "a man who never dies, and who knows everything," and there is certainly something strange about Saint-Germain's widely reported failure to age. Countess von Georgy, whom Saint-Germain so surprised when they met again in 1760, stated that in Venice in 1710, the count had given her an "elixir" that for a quarter of a century preserved the beauty she possessed at the age of 25.

If there is an explanation for all this, it probably lies in Saint-Germain's ability as an alchemist. Everywhere he went he set up an elaborate laboratory, and he was renowned for his prodigious scientific knowledge. When Richard Chanfray maintained on French television in 1972 that he was the still-living Saint-Germain, he "proved" his point by apparently turning lead into gold in front of the cameras. And it is fundamental to alchemical lore that success in performing this operation is accompanied by the blessing of eternal physical life — immortality.

Contemporary alchemist

Saint-Germain is not the only person alleged to have discovered the secret of eternal life through alchemy. There is, for example, the mysterious Fulcanelli, author of a series of occult books published in Paris in the 1920's. Those who knew him personally — notably his former pupil, Eugene Cansaliet — said that Fulcanelli was elderly, rich, enormously erudite, and possibly of noble lineage, but that he refused to divulge his true identity. Cansaliet claimed that, on one occasion, Fulcanelli had given him a minute quantity of what he called "powder of projection" that, added to four ounces of molten lead, turned it into pure gold.

Cansaliet last worked with Fulcanelli when the alchemist was 80. Thirty years were to pass before the two met again, at a castle in the mountains near Seville, Spain. But, said Cansaliet, Fulcanelli looked like a man of 50, although his true age must have been nearer 110. In 1981 Cansaliet, then aged 80 himself, claimed to have met Fulcanelli again on several occasions; but he had observed that Fulcanelli had gradually taken on the appearance of a woman. This, according to the literature of alchemy, is one of the more bizarre side effects of success in the Great Work, as the alchemist himself gradually becomes a perfect being, neither male nor female, but androgynous.

Could Saint-Germain and Fulcanelli possibly have shared the same elusive alchemical knowledge? Whatever the reality of their strange and long lives, they were certainly both intriguing and charismatic characters.

THE ALCHEMISTS

Originating with the Arabs in Egypt some 1,400 years ago, alchemy was a form of mystical chemistry that, its practitioners claimed, held the secret of turning base metals, such as lead and tin, into pure gold. The alleged key to the alchemists' power was the philosopher's stone, a potent substance also known as the universal solvent, which was supposed to effect the magical transmutation of matter.

Lust for gold

Throughout the Middle Ages, the alchemist was a powerful, mysterious figure, courted by the princes of Europe greedy for an inexhaustible source of wealth. Of course alchemy never actually worked, but the promise of free gold was too alluring to resist, even after repeated disappointments.

Gradually, over the years, alchemy took on a more spiritual quality, without losing any of its mysterious aura. The philosopher's stone was identified with the elixir of life, and the making of gold came to be viewed as only a symbol of the alchemist's true pursuit — immortality.

Eternal life

Inevitably, the secret of eternal life was found to be just as elusive as the secret of

Alchemical images

The secret "science" of alchemy generated a rich symbolism to express its arcane knowledge. The figure of the androgyne, both male and female in one body, was especially significant in alchemical lore.

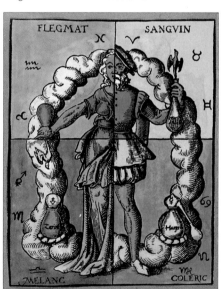

creating gold. But it also proved equally irresistible, and many a fortune was sunk in the tortuous quest for the fabulous elixir that could defeat age and death.

Hidden truths

The magical practice of alchemy largely died out with the dawn of the modern scientific age 300 years ago. Some researchers still believe, however, that although many alchemists were undoubtedly charlatans, others had genuinely been on the track of hidden truths that may yet be confirmed by the progress of science.

THE MARKS OF CHRIST

Stigmata are repetitions of the wounds believed to have been suffered by Christ at His Crucifixion: the holes made by the nails in His hands and feet, by the crown of thorns on His forehead, and by the spear in His side.

THE CRUCIFIXION

Historians have argued that the wounds exhibited by stigmatics do not, in fact, correspond with the actual wounds of the Crucifixion.

Medieval stigmatic

Historical evidence suggests that the Roman method of crucifixion was to tie the arms to the cross with ropes and then to drive nails through the wrists. So the stigmata may in fact accord with the wounds shown in Renaissance paintings and in church statuary, rather than with the actual method that we now understand would have been used for a crucifixion at the time of Christ's execution. They may correspond to the *idea* of Christ's wounds, rather than the reality.

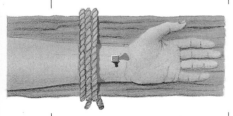

Roman crucifixion

INEXPLICABLY, FROM THE FIRST recorded case of stigmatization — that of St. Francis of Assisi in 1224 — to the present day, hundreds of people have been marked with these replicas of the wounds of Christ's Passion.

Why — and how — does it happen? Can deeply devout Christians really share in Christ's sufferings simply by meditating on them? Is stigmatization a strange clinical condition, in some way akin to hysteria? Or is it, in fact, no more than a particularly clever hoax?

There is probably no simple answer. The Catholic Church treats cases of stigmatization with great skepticism, and earlier this century ordered stigmatic Padre Pio to keep out of the public eye. While psychiatrists term it psychologically induced bleeding, the church believes there are three possible explanations: divine revelation; the work of the devil to confuse the faithful; or conscious or unconscious suggestion. But no one theory works for all the great variety of known cases.

Christ on the cross
A crucifix showing the wounds that the stigmata mimic.

Cloretta Robinson

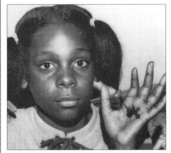

The case of Cloretta Robinson, a Baptist from West Oakland, California, is unusual in that she is the first known non-Catholic stigmatic. At the age of 10, in 1972, she developed stigmata for several days over Easter. She was examined by two doctors, neither of whom could find any medical explanation for the blood that appeared on her hands, feet, left side, and forehead.

Antonio Ruffino

In 1951 Antonio Ruffino saw an apparition of the Virgin Mary and received the stigmata. To mark the visitation, Ruffino built a chapel on the site, south of Rome. He subsequently bled from his hands and feet for over 40 years.

Padre Pio

A model of piety and humility and probably the most venerated of modern-day stigmatics, Padre Pio was laid to rest in southern Italy in 1968. A Capuchin monk, he had bled continually for over 50 years. He hid his wounds from public gaze, staying within the walls of the monastery of San Giovanni Rotondo in Foggia, and appeared in public only to say Mass (right). His stigmata first appeared in 1918, just three days after the Capuchins had celebrated the Feast of the Stigmata of St. Francis of Assisi.

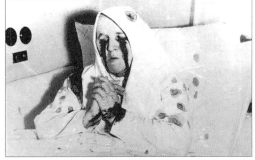

"Pope Gregory"

Clemente Dominguez, from Palmar de Troya in Spain, proclaimed himself Pope Gregory XVIII in the late 1970's, and periodically developed the wounds of Christ's Passion, including a chest wound and the marks of the crown of thorns. Dominguez claimed to have had heavenly visions each night since being blinded in a car accident in 1976. In contrast to Padre Pio, Dominguez openly flaunted his wounds and reveled in the devotion of his followers.

FRANCIS OF ASSISI

St. Francis of Assisi is the first person recorded to have developed stigmata. His stigmatization occurred in 1224. He was praying outside his spiritual retreat, a cave in the Apennines, when he saw a winged seraph in the skies and fell into a swoon. According to contemporary accounts, the stigmata appeared as he struggled to his feet and called for help. In the words of his biographer, Thomas Celano, writing in 1226: "His hands and feet seemed pierced in the midst by nails, the heads of the nails appearing in the inner part of the hands and in the upper part of the feet, and their points over against them.... Moreover his right side, as if it had been pierced by a lance, was overlaid with a scar, and often shed forth blood...."

Teresa Neumann

Born in Bavaria in 1898, Teresa Neumann was bedridden, blind, and paralyzed by the age of 20, apparently as a result of a hysterical reaction to a fire at a neighboring farm. A few years later, she had a vision of St. Theresa of Lisieux, after which her afflictions were suddenly cured and she herself developed stigmata. For over 30 years, until her death in 1962, she suffered Christ's Passion every Friday. Each week, on that day, wounds appeared in her hands, feet, and side, and she wept blood-tinged tears, sometimes losing nearly a pint of blood. However, she was always well again by Sunday, the wounds miraculously healing by then. The authenticity of her stigmata was vigorously challenged throughout her life, but fraud was never proved.

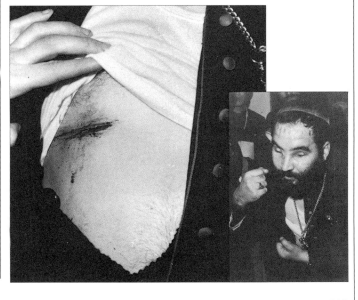

INTRUSIONS FROM ELSEWHERE

THERE MAY BE FEW CLAIMANTS to physical immortality, but there are hosts of others who will attest to the survival of the personality after death. By no means do all do so from religious conviction: they take their stand on the evidence that some dead people have communicated quite convincingly with those who are still alive. But these apparent communications can sometimes occur in the most disturbing fashion.

Spirit control
In July 1877, 13-year-old Lurancy Vennum of Watseka, Illinois, had a seizure and announced that she could see heaven and angels, as well as people whom she had known but who were now dead. Her startled and

When Lurancy saw her real family during this time, she treated them as strangers.

distressed family eventually took the advice of their neighbors, Mr. and Mrs. Roff, and called in Dr. E. W. Stevens of Janesville, Wisconsin. Mr. Roff brought Dr. Stevens to see Lurancy in January 1878. By this time she was in a state of constant inner turmoil. The doctor succeeded in calming her, only to hear her say that a spirit called Mary Roff wanted to take control of her. Mr. Roff exclaimed "That is my daughter; Mary Roff is my girl. Why, she has been in heaven 12 years. Yes, let her come, we'll be glad to have her come." Mary Roff had also suffered from dreadful seizures and she finally died in 1865 at the age of 18 following a particularly terrible fit. Now, it seemed, her spirit wanted to return to this life by possessing Lurancy Vennum's physical body. From that time, Lurancy — or Mary Roff — began to demand to "go home to her parents," and on February 11, 1878, she did so. Once inside the Roffs' house, she immediately recognized clothes, belongings, friends, and relatives, and talked familiarly about events from Mary's past that had occurred up to 25 years previously, before Lurancy

A girl possessed
Lurancy Vennum was 13 years old when she was allegedly possessed by the spirit of a dead neighbor, Mary Roff.

was born. When Lurancy saw her real family during this time, she treated them as complete strangers.

Then, on May 7, "Mary Roff" sat down, closed her eyes, opened them, and said: "Where am I? I was never here before." Lurancy had apparently reappeared in her own body. But five minutes later, she was behaving like Mary Roff again, and continued to alternate between the two personalities until May 21, when "Mary" announced that it was time for Lurancy to return, and said good-bye to the Roff family.

Lurancy happily returned home, and only on rare and brief occasions after that did the spirit of Mary Roff return to disturb her. Skeptics point out that Lurancy may have picked up the knowledge of the Roff household that she displayed as "Mary" from conversations between the Roffs and her own parents. Without consciously logging the fact that she had heard these details, they may have been stored in her memory. A genuine mental disturbance may have brought forth a secondary personality capable of fastening on to this unconscious material. But we cannot rule out the possibility that, in some sense, Mary Roff really did take over Lurancy Vennum's body for a time.

Outback physician
The more recent case of British medium Thomas Fox provides remarkably convincing evidence that possession is not just a product of the "victim's" mind.

In the late 1960's a medium named Billy Elton said that one of Fox's spirit guides — the spiritual entities through whom a medium makes contact with other spirit forms — was an Australian called Dr. Tester. Fox had never heard, seen, or sensed the spirit of such a

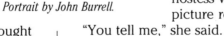

A psychic artist had painted the picture of Doc Tester several years before.

Doc Tester
Portrait by John Burrell.

person at all and thought no more about it. But at a séance a year or two later, Jack Toyer, a developing medium, told him, in a somewhat disapproving voice: "Tom....There's a spirit form, of an old Mexican in a big black hat, standing behind you, you know."

"Well, I don't know who he is," said Fox, "but he's welcome."

Soon after this, Fox himself went into a trance and in a voice not his own boomed out: "Who the bloody hell d'ye think you're calling an old Mexican? I'm no old Mexican, mate. My name's Doc Tester." Then, through Fox, Doc Tester launched into a long talk about healing. After this, Fox heard no more from, or about, Tester for years.

In the early 1970's Fox was invited to the house of some new friends for tea. When he arrived, the first thing he saw was an oil painting of a man dressed in black, with black hair, and a wide-brimmed black hat. At once he asked his hostess whom the picture represented.

"You tell me," she said.

"His name's Doc Tester, he's Australian, and he worked in the outback," Fox heard himself saying before he had a chance to think.

"He's been waiting here three years for you," said his hostess.

Fox was completely amazed. How could anyone else know about Doc Tester? How had anyone been able to paint this picture, or be sure that he would get to know about it? Then the story came out.

John Burrell, a psychic artist, had painted the picture several years before. There were two unusual things about his art. He only painted portraits of the dead, whom he had never seen in the flesh or in photographs, and he always painted with his eyes closed, in a state of trance.

THE SLEEPING PROPHET
Psychic doctor Edgar Cayce was born on a Kentucky farm in 1877 and died in 1945. While in a trance he was apparently able to answer questions about the past, dwelling extensively on the role of the lost civilization of Atlantis and its importance in the evolution of humankind. Many of his readings relating to the past give extensive detail regarding the location of numerous historic sites, but as yet none of these has been subject to the serious archeological research necessary to verify his claims.

Alarming revelations
Like Nostradamus in 16th-century France, Cayce made predictions regarding the future, and there are those who claim that many have been proved accurate. His devotees believe that he foresaw the two World Wars, the 1929 Wall Street crash, the discovery of the Dead Sea Scrolls, and the invention of lasers. Among his many predictions is an alarming claim regarding a massive upheaval in the world due to come about around the year 2000. This would result in major geographical changes, including the destruction of Los Angeles and San Francisco by massive earthquakes. During a prophetic dream he had in 1936, Cayce flew over a destroyed city in the process of being rebuilt. On asking the name of the city he was told: "New York."

It will not be long, therefore, before we will all be able to judge the authenticity of Cayce's predictions for ourselves.

Among the pictures of spirit guides he painted was a portrait in oil of a black-haired man, who was wearing a black hat. He looked a bit like a character from a western, except that in the background of the picture there were sheep, not longhorn steers.

"It's not yours," he had said when he gave it away, "and it's not for you. But hang it on your wall. This is an Australian doctor, and he's somebody's healer in spirit. Someone will be along eventually to collect it."

Dust from the bush
Today the painting hangs in Fox's consulting room in London. Fox is convinced that Tester has, indeed, done spiritual healing through him, guiding his physical actions while he is in a state of trance. Fox says that he has since found out that Tester was an ordinary country doctor, working in the Australian outback in the 1920's. Tester would spend weeks at a time riding from station to station and from settlement to settlement on horseback — which accounts for his scruffy attire: he wears old clothes, which are covered with dust from his journeys in the bush.

Thomas Fox

The most remarkable part of this story is that three mediums besides Fox himself independently either saw or were aware of Doc Tester, two of them before Fox himself had known anything about his spirit guide; and the man who painted Tester's picture was someone whom Fox had never met. But are we really to believe Doc Tester is a spirit, or is he perhaps a figure from Fox's unconscious which the other mediums were "tuning into" telepathically? Or is there another explanation?

Psychic consultant
One theory was suggested by Edgar Cayce, one of the most famous psychic healers of all time. In preparation for what he called a reading, Cayce would loosen his clothes and make himself comfortable on his couch. He would then close his eyes and start to breathe deeply and evenly. Once in this trancelike state, Cayce would be told the name and location of his subject.

Despite the large distances that often separated healer and patient, Cayce was apparently able to visualize the patients, describe what he thought their illnesses were, and then prescribe suitable treatments. Between 1901 and 1945 he gave thousands of readings, many of them for people he had never met, correctly diagnosing their illnesses and prescribing cures. A huge archive of these readings is on record at the Association for Research and Enlightenment, an organization which was founded by Cayce in 1934, in Virginia Beach, Virginia.

Cayce was frequently called the Sleeping Prophet because he always worked in a trance. He believed that the information he received was so accurate because he had the gift of paranormal access to the "Akashic records." This term comes from the Sanskrit word *akasha*, which means "the fundamental etheric substance of the universe." These records are allegedly a repository of everything that has been said and done since the beginning of time.

Time theories
Albert Einstein suggested that time is an eternal "now," through which our lives move in a single, arbitrary direction. Paranormal talents may be the ability to move mentally in other directions through time. If this is true, we are as yet unable to solve the mystery of what it is that gives psychics their peculiar power to navigate across time unconstrained by the rules that govern the rest of us. But such a notion could well explain Cayce's phenomenal accuracy as a psychic healer, the apparent possession of Lurancy Vennum, and the unanimous and unprompted agreement of several psychics on the appearance of Thomas Fox's spirit guide, Doc Tester.

PROPHET OF DOOM

Nostradamus — physician, alchemist, and philosopher — is probably the world's best-known prophet. His predictions have continued to stimulate enormous interest for over 400 years.

ORN MICHEL DE NOSTRADAME on December 14, 1503, in Saint-Rémy, Provence, in the south of France, Nostradamus studied philosophy and medicine, and soon earned a reputation as a great healer during the plague of Montpellier in the 1530's — though, tragically, his wife and children perished in the epidemic.

In 1550 he published his first almanac of prophecies for the coming year. He later wrote a complete series of 10 *Centuries*, written in enigmatic quatrains (four-line verses), predicting world events up until the end of the world in 3797.

Nostradamus's verses are not easy to understand. Nevertheless, they have been interpreted as offering predictions of many major historical events.

Birth of an emperor
The following quatrain (*Centuries* III:35) is supposed to prophesy the birth of Napoleon:
*In the profoundest part of the west of Europe
— A child will be born of a poor family
By his speech he will seduce a great company,
Greater in reputation than in the Kingdom of the East.*

Atomic bombs
This verse (*Centuries* II:6) is held to prophesy the atomic bombing of Hiroshima and Nagasaki:
*Near the harbor and in two cities
Will be two scourges — of which like has not been seen
Hunger, pestilence within, people by sword evicted
Will cry for help from the great immortal God.*

Nostradamus and the queen
Nostradamus's predictions were held in high esteem during his lifetime. Queen Catherine de Medicis and other members of the French royal family courted him assiduously in an effort to unlock the secrets of their destiny.

The rise of Hitler
One of Nostradamus's most famous predictions (*Centuries* II:24) allegedly concerned the emergence of Hitler as the leader of Nazi Germany. As usual with Nostradamus, the prophecy is couched in such general terms that it could apply to many possible situations. But the similarity between the name "Hister" that appears in the prediction and "Hitler" is quite uncanny:
*Beasts wild with hunger will swim across rivers,
The greatest part of the field will oppose Hister
In a cage of iron he will drag the leader
When German offspring knows no law.*

The benefit of hindsight
Detractors have claimed, however, that Nostradamus's prophecies are no more than ambiguous guesswork and that it is only with hindsight that any credibility can be given to his writings. Certainly, no one has succeeded in using his prophecies to foretell precise future events. But they remain an intriguing enigma.

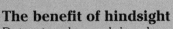
Napoleon Bonaparte

CHAPTER FIVE

WINDOWS IN TIME AND SPACE

Einstein's theories have led us to consider time as a dimension like any other. Perhaps the people who tell of finding themselves suddenly in another time or place are travelers in this uncharted dimension?

The late Ivan Sanderson, well-known naturalist, scientist, and researcher of psychic and supernatural phenomena, recounted in his book *More "Things"* the following dramatic example of a timeslip that he himself experienced. While engaged on a biological survey in Haiti, he and his wife found themselves marooned in the jungle one evening when their car broke down. They set off walking along

Ivan Sanderson
Before his Haitian experience, Sanderson, an eminent scientist and naturalist, had never taken any great interest in the occult. He did not actively disbelieve in it but he was, as he saw it, far too busy catching up with the "more pragmatic facts of life."

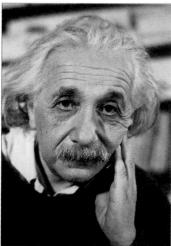

Albert Einstein
Einstein, the father of modern physics, established that time is not a constant. Today most people perceive time as a linear progression. Other theories have been formulated, however, that suggest the possibility of seeing the future before the present.

the road cut through the thick tropical vegetation, in the direction they hoped would eventually lead them home.

A strange vision

Tired and thirsty, and despairing of getting back to their beds that night, Sanderson and his wife simultaneously experienced a strange and vivid vision. Suddenly, the overhanging trees of the jungle transformed themselves into a narrow city street stretching ahead of them. In the bright moonlight Sanderson could make out that the houses were of three stories, overhanging the road, which was cobbled and dotted with large patches of mud. The warm glow of candlelight shone from behind some of the small leaded windows. Although the air was still, lanterns in iron frames hanging from the house fronts swung in unison, as if blown by the wind. Both Sanderson and his wife were convinced that they had been transported to a street in Paris, France, 500 years before.

For several minutes they compared notes and remarked several authentic details of a 15th-century Paris street scene. Then, feeling weak and dizzy, they sat down on what they perceived to be a large, rough curbstone. Abruptly the vision faded, and they found themselves once more back in the jungle.

Some interesting and occasionally disturbing hypotheses have been advanced to explain such odd experiences. The most popular is the void, hole, or window in our world through which a person, creature, or object can pass through into another place, planet,

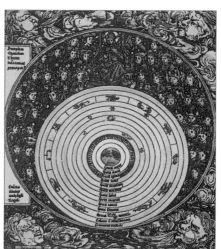

A medieval view of the cosmos
For centuries, it was believed that the earth was at the center of the universe. It may be that our current concept of time will prove to be equally misguided.

time, or dimension of reality. It sounds like science fiction, but physicists have argued that it is theoretically possible for other dimensions of reality to exist.

One of the corollaries of Einstein's theory of relativity is that time is not a constant. It is a fact that an astronaut, for example, sent on a journey at very high speed, ages less than the rest of us left behind on earth. This stretching of time leads us to wonder whether it is possible actually to reverse it.

Recent discoveries in space include the phenomena called black holes, well-like centers of high density that will not even allow light to escape the tremendous force of their gravitational pull. Scientists have speculated that black holes may act as pathways to other universes. The matter flowing into them may be pouring into other regions of space and time of which we have absolutely no knowledge. Who knows what other gateways to strange and distant dimensions may exist?

Windows in space or time could provide the answer to all sorts of anomalous phenomena: ghosts, telepathy, precognitive dreams, out-of-the-body experiences, past lives, disappearances, appearances of strange people and animals, and UFO's. It is possible, for example, that ghostly phenomena could be a glimpse of the past, as seen through one of these "windows." Ghosts are usually dressed in the costume of the period in which they lived, and are sometimes reported to have walked on a former floor level, or through doors that no longer exist. Occasionally the observer so fully

> ## Suddenly, the overhanging trees of the jungle transformed themselves into a narrow city street stretching ahead of them.

enters the phantom's world that the reality of the present vanishes altogether. This too fits neatly into the theory, and would occur when the observer actually passes through the window, rather than merely looking through it.

Precognitive dreams require another shift of the imagination. Current thinking suggests that the dreamer is actually receiving telepathic messages from someone in the future. If this is so, we have to accept that we are not at the tip of the "Arrow of Time," but probably somewhere back along the shaft. Indeed, to assume (as we have done for centuries) that we are in the vanguard of time as it marches steadily forward may prove to be as presumptuous as Aristotle's view of the earth being at the center of the universe.

Reality in parallel

Science fiction gives scientists and others freedom to speculate to a degree denied them elsewhere, and has produced a number of intriguing theories. Parallel worlds, for example, could prove the solution to the problem that arises if the past is altered by a visitor from the future. Parallel worlds would be created every time history was changed, allowing our own world to carry on as before. It has also been suggested that there may be several realities occupying the same spatial coordinates as our own. In these "other worlds," people may have advanced at different rates from us. In this case, sightings of UFO's and monsters of various types may just be fleeting glimpses through the curtain that hangs over the window separating these parallel worlds.

Could an interdimensional window explain the terrifying experience of Thomas B. Cumpston? According to a report in *The Times* of London of December 11, 1873, Cumpston and his wife were an elderly couple who had traveled from their home in Leeds to Bristol, and there spent the night of

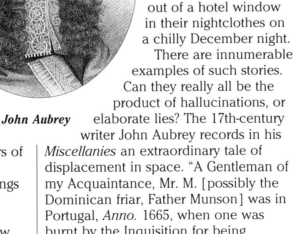

John Aubrey

December 8–9 in the Victoria Hotel. About 4:00 A.M. they were awakened by strange noises. As Cumpston got out of bed, a hole appeared in the floor. He found himself being dragged toward the opening, and it is reported that only the prompt action of his wife in pulling him back from the brink saved him.

The couple fled in their nightclothes to the nearby railway station, where they were arrested. The subsequent police investigation showed the Cumpstons' hotel room to be apparently normal. The police said that they had had a "collective hallucination." If so, it was severe enough to cause a respectable elderly couple to jump out of a hotel window in their nightclothes on a chilly December night.

There are innumerable examples of such stories. Can they really all be the product of hallucinations, or elaborate lies? The 17th-century writer John Aubrey records in his *Miscellanies* an extraordinary tale of displacement in space. "A Gentleman of my Acquaintance, Mr. M. [possibly the Dominican friar, Father Munson] was in Portugal, *Anno.* 1665, when one was burnt by the Inquisition for being brought thither from Goa in East India, in the Air, in an incredible short time." The question remains whether this was a madman or a fool, or, like the Sandersons and the Cumpstons, just another victim who stumbled through a window in time and space.

ANOTHER DIMENSION?

Only recently have scientists sought in earnest to extend the boundaries of our existence, by discovering further dimensions for humankind to explore. But for centuries philosophers and writers have been toying with this concept.

Time traveling

H.G. Wells's book, *The Time Machine*, published in 1895, was one of the earliest to explore the possibilities of travel in a fourth dimension, that of time. Wells himself described his novel as an "assault on human self-satisfaction," for the possibilities raised by time travel merely highlight the complacency of humankind in assuming that it already knows the basic principles that rule the universe.

Flatland

Edwin Abbott's book, *Flatland*, published in 1884, gives an even better example of how each new dimension is incomprehensible until it is physically perceived. In the book, the inhabitants of the one-dimensional Lineland find it impossible to conceive of a two-dimensional place called Flatland, whose inhabitants in turn cannot accept the existence of a three-dimensional region named Spaceland. A denizen of Flatland is baffled by a visit from a sphere from Spaceland; he has no way of understanding where it has come from, being able only to sense in two dimensions.

Borders of fantasy

The obvious analogy is our blinkered view of the universe. We are aware of the existence of four dimensions, but it is possible, suggests Abbott, that there are as many more again. His book highlights an opinion often expressed by the more open-minded researchers into unexplained phenomena. If, they say, like the scientific establishment, we judge data on too narrow a basis, we are likely to remain in the dark forever.

DREAM TIME

If it is possible to dream the future, then it must have already happened. This was the starting point of J.W. Dunne's theory of time, which suggests that within any one human being, there is an infinite series of different selves, each one experiencing time in a different way.

Dunne in an early aircraft

J. W. DUNNE
John William Dunne was born in 1875, the son of a general in the British Army. He followed the same career as his father, and was wounded in action during the Boer War in South Africa in 1900. He was also an aircraft enthusiast during the hazardous early days of flight. In 1907 he designed Britain's first ever military airplane. His fame as a philosopher of time resulted from the publication of his book *An Experiment with Time* in 1927. None of his subsequent works achieved the same renown or popular success. He died in 1949.

IN THE SPRING of 1902 J. W. Dunne, a British infantry officer serving in South Africa, experienced a vivid nightmare. In his dream, he was standing on a mountainous island when jets of steam began to flash out from fissures in the rock. Realizing that the island was in fact a volcano about to explode, Dunne was desperate to save the inhabitants. He appealed in vain to the French authorities to mount an evacuation.

A few days later, while the dream was still fresh in his mind, Dunne opened his copy of the London *Daily Telegraph* to find a news item describing a tragic natural disaster on the French Caribbean island of Martinique. The island's volcano, Mont Pelée, had just erupted causing heavy loss of life.

Fact and fantasy
Such premonitory dreams were not unusual in Dunne's experience. For many years he had slept with a note pad and pencil by his bedside, methodically recording his every dream as soon as he awoke. Time and time again he discovered that the dreams contained elements that turned out to be glimpses of the future, mixed in with memories of his past and fragments of pure fantasy. To Dunne it seemed that the existence of these "dreams of the future" over-turned the whole common sense view of the world of time as a linear progression of past, present, and future. He attacked those who "while willing to concede that we habitually observe events before they occur, suppose that such prevision may be treated as a minor logical difficulty." It was his view, on the contrary, that "If prevision be a fact, it is a fact which destroys absolutely the entire basis of all our past opinions of the universe."

Fixed futures
Dunne attempted to set out a new view of time and consciousness that would account for the premonitory dreams he

> "If prevision be a fact, it is a fact which destroys absolutely the entire basis of all our past opinions of the universe."

was sure he had experienced. His time theory was complex and, some would claim, both confusing and confused. Yet when published as *An Experiment with Time* in 1927, it met with critical acclaim and became a bestseller.

Like many philosophers and scientists in the 20th century, Dunne rejected the everyday common sense idea of time being a succession of moments leading directly from the past into an as yet nonexistent future. He felt that this concept of time was proved by his premonitory dreams to be false. If it was possible to dream of the future, then the future must already exist — it must in some sense have already happened.

Dunne came to the conclusion that what he was able to see in his dreams were not future events themselves, but his own future experience of events. He believed that he had not foreseen the volcanic eruption, for example, but the experience of reading the newspaper article about the eruption. Strong evidence for this view was provided by one striking detail of his Martinique volcano dream. Dunne remembered, in the dream, insisting that the lives of 4,000 people were at risk. According to the newspaper headline he later read, 40,000 people had lost their lives. When Dunne had first glanced through the news story, however, he had misread the headline figure as 4,000. So what had appeared in his dream, he suggested, was a trace of his future misreading of the figure in the newspaper. Neither figure corresponded to the actual number of people killed in the eruption.

Premonitory dreams

Dunne's theoretical solution to the problem of premonitory dreams involved the idea that, within any one individual human being, there is an infinite series of different "selves," each experiencing time in a different way.

To simplify, imagine an individual personality split into two observers. The first observer is like a passenger on a train being carried at a steady rate from the past into the future. Immersed in linear time, he can remember the stations and countryside he has passed through on the journey already, and he can see what is passing outside the window at present. But the track ahead is something he can only discover in the course of time. There is another observer, however, hovering in a helicopter high

---

> ## "The distinction between past, present, and future is an illusion, although a persistent one."
> ### Albert Einstein

---

above the railway track. This second observer can see not only where the train has come from and where it is now, but can also view whatever lies ahead, which, to the train-bound observer, is the invisible future.

Human immortality

In Dunne's view, these two observers both exist within the same person. During waking time, the train-bound observer, enclosed in linear time, blots out the higher view of the observer hovering above. But at night the higher observer's view, with its mix of past, present, and future, is dominant.

His faith in this theory led him to a belief in human immortality. Since part of a human being stands outside the linear time of the clocks, he argued, this part would not die with the time-bound body and brain.

RECORD YOUR DREAMS

Dunne suggested a technique that anyone can use for spotting "dreams of the future":

◆ Keep a pen and note pad by your bedside to record your dreams immediately on waking.

◆ Focus your attention on a single dream incident at a time. This will normally recall more associated dream material.

◆ Write down every detail of your dream at once. You will find that dreams slip out of the memory very easily.

◆ Sometimes it may be difficult to tell whether a dream is about what happened yesterday or tomorrow. Make sure to record your dreams on nights before a sudden change in routine.

◆ Re-read your earlier accounts of dreams at the end of each day. Look for connections with recent happenings. The glimpse of the future may lie in one fragment of a dream story, and will almost certainly be mixed together with other material taken from past experiences or unconnected with any waking experience.

ARRIVALS AND DEPARTURES

The annals of history are full of mysterious appearances and disappearances. Many can be proved never to have happened; many others have the most mundane explanations; a very few are truly baffling.

Lord Stanhope

A NOBLE CAUSE?
An enigma to the general public, Kaspar Hauser was also a mystery to those who knew him well. Some believed he was a genius. Others thought him an imbecile. To the eccentric Englishman Lord Stanhope, Kaspar was a human toy who could be used to entertain his friends.

Paul von Feuerbach

Stanhope may have adopted Kaspar to help the grand duke of Baden hide the secret of Kaspar's identity. Rumor had it that Kaspar was a son of the house of Baden, spirited away at birth and replaced by a dead peasant baby.

Two suspicious deaths
Stanhope tried to quash this story, but the rumors persisted. A friend of Kaspar, the eminent criminologist Paul von Feuerbach, tried to prove his noble birth but died before he could do so. Many say he was poisoned. Like Kaspar himself, Feuerbach took a secret to the grave.

THERE ARE NUMEROUS STORIES, several well documented, of the sudden appearance of people and animals in settings where they are strange and out of place. These are sometimes cited as supporting evidence for the theory that it is possible to slip through an interdimensional window from one time, or from one place, to another. The most famous case of sudden, incongruous appearance is that of Kaspar Hauser.

On the afternoon of Whitmonday, May 26, 1828, a teenage boy hobbled into Unschlitt Square in the Bavarian city of Nuremberg and approached a cobbler named Georg Weichmann. He showed him an envelope that was addressed to "The Captain of the 4th Squadron, 6th Cavalry Regiment, in Nuremberg." The captain's name was Wessenig, and the boy was taken to his house.

Bizarre behavior
Capt. Wessenig was not in. While the boy waited for him to return, his bizarre behavior drew the attention of the captain's servants. He tried to pick up the flame of a candle with his bare fingers, and cried out with astonishment when he was burned. He was terrified almost out of his wits by the chiming of a grandfather clock. The smell of cooking food disgusted him, and he refused all nourishment except bread and water.

Kaspar continued to behave incongruously, as if he had never come across the most commonplace objects and situations.

19th-century Nuremberg
This painting shows the German city of Nuremberg as it was in the early 19th century. The photographic representation of the wandering boy is from a popular film by Werner Herzog.

When Capt. Wessenig eventually arrived, the boy presented him with two letters. One, purporting to be from a poor girl, asked the writer of the second to take care of her child until he was 17 years old, then to make sure that he enlisted in his father's cavalry regiment. The second letter appeared to have been written by the recipient of the first and was intended for Capt. Wessenig. The author, who claimed to be a poor laborer, said that he had kept the boy confined indoors all his life.

Both letters were fakes. The handwriting was similar, the paper was the same, and the ink on both was equally fresh. They were not, however, written by the boy, who was able only to write his name — Kaspar Hauser — in a childish scrawl.

Aptitude for learning

Kaspar continued to behave incongruously, as if he had never come across the most commonplace objects and situations. But his aptitude for learning was remarkable, and he was soon able to read, write, and adopt civilized behavior. He then told his own story. He claimed to have been kept in a small, dark room all his life. Bread and water were placed in his cell when he was asleep. Sometimes the water would taste strange and he would fall asleep soon after drinking it. On these occasions he would wake to find his cell cleaned and his hair and nails cut. The only person he had ever seen was a man who one day came into his room and taught him to write his name and to pronounce a few simple phrases. This man had later led him upstairs to daylight and taken him to the outskirts of Nuremberg.

The sudden appearance of such an enigma caused a sensation throughout

A forged letter

Kaspar was carrying two letters when he was found. This one is written as if from his mother, asking the recipient to look after the boy until he reached the age of 17. The other letter was supposed to be from the recipient of the first, written a number of years later. However, both were in the same handwriting and written in the same ink.

the city. There was much speculation about where he had come from and who he might really be. The controversy became even more intense when, on

Kaspar was found unconscious. He had been attacked by a stranger wearing a silken mask.

October 7, 1829, Kaspar was found unconscious in the cellar of the house in which he lived. He claimed that he had been attacked by a stranger wearing a silken mask.

The authorities now moved Kaspar into the care of the criminologist and

legal expert Paul Johann Anselm Ritter von Feuerbach. He was convinced of Kaspar's noble birth and pronounced that: "Kaspar Hauser is the legitimate son of royal parents and was put out of the way to open succession to other heirs."

In May 1831 an eccentric English nobleman, Lord Charles Stanhope, began to take a keen interest in Kaspar,

126

Kaspar's paintings
Kaspar produced these two watercolors of a flower and some fruit. Each has his signed visiting-card inserted in the corner of the frame.

adopted him, and moved him to nearby Ansbach. Here, on December 14, 1833, Kaspar was stabbed while walking in the park. The wound, though superficial, proved fatal, and Kaspar died just three days later.

A royal changeling?

Kaspar's murder fueled yet more speculation about his origin. The most popular theory was that he was the legitimate heir to a very high position, possibly the grand duke of Baden.

Others said he was a fraud. How did he come to have a healthy complexion when he first appeared, if he had spent his entire life in a darkened cell? they asked. They even went as far as to suggest that he had staged the attacks himself in order to reawaken public interest in his story.

Kaspar's amazing tale may not have been entirely true. But we do know that his feet were badly blistered when he first arrived in Nuremberg. And what motive could he possibly have had for such an elaborate charade?

The Green Children

An even more mysterious tale of sudden and incongruous appearance concerns the Green Children of Woolpit in Suffolk, England. This strange tale was told by two medieval chroniclers, Ralph of Coggeshall and William of Newburgh.

One autumn during the reign of King Stephen (A.D.1135–54), some harvesters came upon two children, a boy and a girl, in a ditch. They were "clad in garments of a strange hue and unknown texture," but the most remarkable thing about them was their green skins. In his account, Ralph of Coggeshall added that nobody could understand their language. They were taken to the home of Sir Richard de Calne at Wikes, where they wept bitterly and refused all food except green beans.

Kaspar's coat
This coat is the one Kaspar was wearing when he was fatally stabbed while walking in the park in Ansbach. The gash made by the murder weapon is ringed in this photograph.

Church banner
The tiny village of Woolpit in Suffolk, England, has a long but uneventful history. The sudden appearance of the Green Children is commemorated on a banner in St. Mary's Church, and in the design of the market cross in the center of the village.

Market cross at Woolpit

The boy died within a few weeks, but the girl survived, gradually lost her green hue, and spent several years as a servant in the household of Sir Richard. She was said to be "rather loose and wanton in her conduct," but eventually she married, and the course of the rest of her life is unknown and will, no doubt, remain so.

According to her story, she and the boy had lived in a green, twilight world that they called St. Martin's Land. Just before they were found, they had been transported from there in some kind of magical manner.

An analysis of this story yields some interesting points. The estate at Wikes certainly existed, and records show that there was a family named "de Calna" there in the 12th century. William of Newburgh was well acquainted with the gullibility of fellow chroniclers, and freely admits that at first he refused to believe the tale: "I thought it ridiculous...until I was overwhelmed with the weight of so many and such credible witnesses." Ralph of Coggeshall

She and the boy had lived in a green, twilight world called St. Martin's Land.

claimed to have gone as far as to interview Sir Richard de Calne and his family, who confirmed the story.

It seems most likely, however, that the country people might simply have embroidered a story about the discovery of two ordinary stray children. In medieval times green was regarded as a supernatural color, and green beans were also thought to have special properties. It is also the favored color of aliens in science fiction, which may be reflected in the sightings of "little green men," a common phenomenon of the last 40 years.

Arriving by UFO?
Archbishop Agobard of Lyons in France tells another story of people from unknown lands. In his 9th-century *Liber de Grandine et Tonitruis*, he tells of four "cloud sailors" from a land called Magonia. Agobard came upon a mob about to kill three men and a woman whom they claimed had descended from "aerial ships," and whom they thought were sorcerers. "In vain," writes Agobard, "the four innocents sought to vindicate themselves by saying that they were of their own countryfolk, and had been carried away a short time since by miraculous men who had shown them unheard-of marvels."

Agobard was not in the slightest awed by the claims of either the four strangers or the startled townspeople of Lyons. He calmly announced with great authority that the strangers' story was obviously a lie. He added that the townspeople

THE UFO CONNECTION

In the last 50 years, a new explanation has been suggested for some of the more baffling cases of appearance and disappearance.

OVER THE CENTURIES, people have advanced many theories to explain mysterious events, and these reflect the preoccupations of each age. In ancient times such events were thought to be the work of the gods; more recently, elves and fairies were often said to be involved. Since 1947, when the first "flying saucer" was sighted, most reports of mysterious arrivals and departures have involved visitors from other planets.

Abduction!
On November 5, 1975, Travis Walton, a young forestry worker from Snowflake, Arizona, was taken on a strange journey. As he was on his way to work with five companions, they became aware of a bright light hovering over their truck. The driver stopped, and Walton went to investigate. Suddenly there was a flash of light, and he fell to the ground. The driver panicked and drove away. When his fellow workers returned to the spot, the light had gone — and so had Walton.

Sci-fi fantasy
The ancient city of Angkor in Cambodia suffered a massive loss of population in the early 15th century. This dramatic reconstruction from a 1930's sci-fi magazine illustrates one of the more outlandish explanations that have been advanced: that a fleet of spaceships arrived one day and abducted the whole population.

For five days vast tracts of the Arizona desert and forest were combed for any sign of him. His companions were questioned thoroughly by the police, but they appeared to be telling the truth about his disappearance.

Travis Walton

Finally, Walton reappeared in Heber, a small town close to Snowflake. He was scared and dazed, but when he recovered, he told an amazing story. Apparently, after being knocked unconscious by the light, he had been abducted by fetus-like alien creatures in a spaceship. After they had examined him thoroughly, they had replaced him on earth — five days later and several miles away from the abduction site.

The Cergy-Pontoise affair
A similar case of abduction was reported from France, in December 1979. Very early one morning, in Cergy-Pontoise, near Paris, Franck Fontaine and his two friends, Salomon N'Diaye and Jean-Pierre Prévost, were loading up their car, preparing to go to a market.

Prévost saw a UFO in the sky, and pointed it out to N'Diaye. Fontaine was sitting in the car some distance away. Suddenly his two friends saw Fontaine and the vehicle enveloped in a ball of light. They said they saw a light-beam shoot up into the sky, and Fontaine was gone. They reported to the police that he had been abducted by aliens.

The case caused a sensation. Here at last was a UFO abduction with witnesses.

A week later, Fontaine returned. He said that he awoke in a cabbage field near the spot where he was abducted. Not realizing what had happened, he assumed that the car had been stolen. He went straight to the apartment of his friends. He was astonished to discover that he had been away so long.

At first, he could remember nothing of this period of missing time. Later, some confused memories surfaced of having been aboard a spaceship. He suspected that the extraterrestrials had imposed a "block" on his mind to prevent him recalling any details.

Franck Fontaine

Emperor Francis I of Austria
Bathurst's dangerous mission was to the court of the Austrian emperor Francis I at Vienna. This portrait was painted in 1832, three years before the Austrian emperor's death, by Friedrich von Amerling.

Benjamin Bathurst
The disappearance of the young diplomat remains a complete mystery. Whatever actually happened to him that night, Bathurst was certainly taking an enormous risk by exposing himself to the anger of the most powerful man in early 19th-century Europe, Napoleon Bonaparte.

could not possibly have seen them descend from the sky because such a thing was impossible. The four were duly released, and, we may imagine, beat a very hasty departure.

The spy who wasn't there

Another tale of disappearance concerns Benjamin Bathurst, a relative of Earl Bathurst, Foreign Secretary in the British government in 1809. There is no doubt that this case happened, being something of a *cause célèbre* at the time, with a wealth of corroborating details.

Because of his connections in the government, Bathurst was chosen to undertake a dangerous political mission to the court of Emperor Francis I of Austria. Bathurst went to Vienna to urge Austria to join the war against Napoleon. He succeeded, but by October 1809 the Austrians had been defeated in battle and had concluded a peace treaty with Napoleon.

A two-man bodyguard

His mission over, Bathurst set off for England, fearing reprisals from the French. On November 25, 1809, a very nervous Bathurst reached the small German town of Perleberg.

As soon as Bathurst had checked into the White Swan Inn, he paid a call on the commanding officer of the soldiers stationed in the town, Capt. Klitzing. He told the captain that he feared for his life, and asked for immediate protection. The captain duly sent over a bodyguard of two men to the inn.

Vanished into the night

At 7:00 P.M. Bathurst began to make preparations to leave the town. He dismissed the guard and ordered fresh horses. What happened next is not altogether clear from contemporary accounts, but it seems that Bathurst stood outside the inn watching his portmanteau being loaded onto the carriage. He stepped out of the light as he walked around the heads of the horses — and was never seen again.

At first light Capt. Klitzing had the river dragged and the outhouses, woods, ditches, and marshes searched. No trace of Bathurst was found. A few weeks later his trousers were discovered outside the town, with two bullet holes in them — but with no sign of blood.

The disappearance of this young nobleman in such mysterious circumstances caused quite a stir. A large reward was offered for information, but none was forthcoming. Napoleon himself swore on his honor that he had played no part in Bathurst's strange disappearance, and encouraged the latter's relatives to make any inquiries they wished in Europe.

No sound of a scuffle

How could a man have been spirited away by robbers or French agents without even a cry or a scuffle being heard by any of the half-dozen people standing around the carriage as it prepared to leave? Is it likely that a man in an extreme state of terror would venture beyond the security of the light from the inn and the sight of his traveling companions? These are the puzzling questions asked by those seeking to bring this tale into the supernatural realm. But the fate of the unfortunate nobleman remains a mystery, and is unlikely ever to be solved. Common sense tells us that Bathurst must have been murdered by robbers or his enemies, yet he was surrounded by witnesses who heard and saw nothing.

BEASTS FROM THE BEYOND

Cryptozoology, the "science of hidden animals," investigates the creatures that appear where and when they are least expected.

EVERY YEAR, ALL OVER the world, seemingly normal, responsible members of society claim to see animals that are either "known" not to exist or to live in areas other than where they are sighted. Large apelike creatures, wolves and huge wild cats in the suburbs, even monsters in freshwater lakes, are reliably reported by a number of witnesses.

A further puzzling fact is that experienced hunters, using all the latest technology, including helicopters, have searched for these monsters immediately after some sightings and have failed to discover anything. No skeletal or other remains of these strange creatures are ever found.

Supporters of the theory of windows in time and space find this anomaly easy to explain. Obviously, they say, these animals are merely glimpsed through the interdimensional curtain and do not exist in our own space-time continuum at all. Other authorities tend to scrutinize the evidence more closely.

Perhaps the most famous of all these creatures is an apelike humanoid that goes by many different names. To Americans he is Bigfoot or Sasquatch, the Russians call him Alma, and in the Himalayas he is known as the Yeti.

Huge footprints

Bigfoot is reputed to be covered in reddish-brown hair and to stand between 6 and 10 feet tall, walking on two legs. He has a receding forehead and almost no neck. Numerous huge footprints have been found, and over 2,000 sightings have now been recorded, in nearly every state in the United States, and even in New York City.

One of the best-documented appearances of Bigfoot occurred in 1967. Roger Patterson, a rancher, and an Indian friend went hunting for Bigfoot at Bluff Creek in northern California. They both saw a female Bigfoot emerge into a clearing, less than 400 feet away from them, and then lope into the forest. The color film they shot of the event has since been exhaustively examined and has never been proved a fake.

The Loch Ness monster

In Scotland, the Loch Ness monster is another example of a mysterious beast that has eluded capture by man. Although the monster has frequently been sighted, innumerable expeditions, over many decades, have failed to find any solid proof of "Nessie's" existence.

Are there really wondrous creatures in our midst? The window theory says that they are indeed real but simply do not live in our dimension. Perhaps the creatures do not exist at all and are merely hallucinations or hoaxes. If they are real, how much longer can they elude us in a world whose wildernesses are being eroded every day?

Bigfoot
Investigator René Dahinden beside a sculptural representation of Bigfoot at Willow Creek, California. The sculpture, by Jim McClarin, is eight feet tall.

VISION AT VERSAILLES

If windows in time are all around us why do they open for some people but not for others? Why, for instance, should two levelheaded, well-educated, middle-aged Edwardian ladies have been chosen to pass through the barrier of time, to witness the lives of courtiers who had been dead for over a hundred years?

NE AUGUST AFTERNOON in 1901, two sprightly English ladies, Miss Anne Moberley and Miss Eleanor Jourdain, were visiting the Palace of Versailles while on vacation in France. Both ladies shared an interest in history and had some academic standing: Miss Moberley was the principal of St. Hugh's College, Oxford, and Miss Jourdain was headmistress of a school outside London.

After touring the palace, they had set off in search of the Petit Trianon, a seven-roomed pavilion built in the grounds by Louis XV and given by his successor, Louis XVI, to his wife, Queen Marie Antoinette. It was here, wearing rustic dress, that the queen liked to play at being a milkmaid with her ladies in waiting.

Two gardeners busy at work seemed oddly clad, in long gray-green coats and three-cornered hats.

The Petit Trianon was proving difficult to find, and soon the two ladies were lost. The sultry afternoon was starting to have a strange effect on them — inducing a feeling of almost dreamlike melancholy. Nothing seemed quite real. Two gardeners were busy at work, and although they seemed oddly clad, in long gray-green coats and three-cornered hats, neither of the ladies thought to question why these workmen should have been masquerading in 18th-century dress. When asked for directions, the gardeners told them to go straight on.

Strange sensations

As they walked on, both ladies began to feel weighed down by some inexplicable sadness, while it seemed that the landscape around them had taken on a "flat" two-dimensional appearance, reminiscent of theatrical scenery. Their feeling that nothing was quite real was further heightened as their path took them close to a small

---

The women's march
This 19th-century painting by Val Prinsep shows the revolutionary women leading Marie Antoinette and her two children back to Paris.

LAST DAY AT THE PALACE

On October 5, 1789, as famine gripped France, the women of Paris marched the 12 miles to Versailles to demand bread from King Louis XVI himself.

That afternoon was like any other at the palace. The king had gone shooting, while the queen spent the afternoon in the garden of the Petit Trianon.

Awesome mob

When the mob arrived, its number had swelled to 7,000, many of whom were armed with makeshift weapons. The king ordered that every piece of bread in the palace should be given to the women, but this did not satisfy them. They were intent on venting their anger on Marie Antoinette, who was reviled for her rumored extravagance. At 5:30 A.M. the next day a group of women broke in and decapitated two guards before heading for the queen's apartments shouting "Death to the whore!" Marie Antoinette fled, dressed only in a petticoat.

"Take them to Paris!"

The king and queen finally had to confront the mob. Hoping to prevent further bloodshed, they agreed to be taken to Paris. Louis put his trust, he said, in the love of his good subjects. But his subjects had no love left for the man they viewed as a tyrant — on January 21, 1793, he was beheaded on the guillotine, and nine months afterwards Marie Antoinette suffered the same fate.

The phantom queen
This dramatic visualization shows the scene on the terrace of the Petit Trianon as experienced by Miss Moberley on August 10, 1901. The woman has been identified as Marie Antoinette, who has also appeared to other visitors to the Trianon. Did the queen's violent death somehow "fix" her memory for all time in a place where she had once been so happy?

The inset pictures show Miss Jourdain (above) and Miss Moberley (below).

Marie Antoinette
Marie Antoinette, born in 1755, was the daughter of the Habsburg emperor Francis I and the empress Maria Theresa of Austria. At 15 she was married to the French dauphin Louis, and four years later she became queen of France. She was at one time considered the loveliest sovereign in Europe. By the time of her death on the guillotine, however, on October 16, 1793, she was a frail, wizened, white-haired woman, although only 38 years old.

garden pavilion, or summerhouse, in which a swarthy, sinister-looking man was seated. He wore a black cloak with a sombrero-style hat shading his face.

Suddenly they heard the sound of footsteps as someone ran up to them. As Miss Moberley recalled later, this man, in contrast to the one they had seen in the summerhouse, was "distinctly a gentleman" — tall and handsome with black curly hair. He also wore a dark cloak and a sombrero-style hat. He spoke with some urgency, and directed the ladies to the house. Miss Jourdain, who had a good grasp of French, thought his accent curious. As quickly as he had appeared he seemed to disappear into thin air again.

They now crossed a bridge over a man-made ravine, into which gushed a small waterfall, and they found themselves in the garden of the Petit Trianon. A lady was seated on the terrace that ran around the building. She seemed to be busy sketching. She was wearing a long, pale green dress with a low-cut fichu neckline topped off with a white hat. As they passed, the woman looked them straight in the face. Miss Moberley wrote later that although she was quite pretty, there was something rather haggard about her appearance.

The ladies passsed her without speaking, and Miss Moberley felt herself in the grip of an unpleasant sensation, as if walking in a dream. Then she glimpsed the lady again, this time from behind, and she experienced a sensation of relief that Miss Jourdain had not stopped to speak to her. Miss Jourdain, as it turned out, had not seen her at all.

Spirits revived
A young footman then appeared who directed them to the entrance of the Petit Trianon. There they found themselves in the midst of a wedding party, the presence of which did much to revive their spirits. When they felt their equilibrium was restored, they returned to their hotel.

It was not until a full week later that the two ladies actually discussed what they had experienced at Versailles. Miss Moberley asked Miss Jourdain if she thought the Petit Trianon was haunted, and Miss Jourdain replied that yes, she did. The two began to compare notes and found that their perception of events differed quite considerably. In particular, Miss Jourdain had not seen the woman on the terrace, although she had felt the presence of someone near to that spot and had actually pulled her skirt out of the way as she passed. One thing both agreed on, however, was that the place had a very strange, oppressive atmosphere.

Miss Moberley felt herself in the grip of an unpleasant sensation, as if she was walking in a dream.

Their curiosity whetted, the two women returned several times to Versailles. There they were unable to retrace their steps. Everything had changed: the summerhouse did not appear to be the same building; there was no one dressed in 18th-century fashion; there was no sense of eeriness; the woods and paths had gone; the ravine, the bridge, and the waterfall had all disappeared. In other words, the 20th-century reality appeared to bear little resemblance to the scene they had originally witnessed.

Intrigued, the two ladies undertook to research the history of the Trianon and found much evidence to support their theory that they had slipped back to the world of Marie Antoinette. They concluded that the sinister-looking

man they had seen in the summerhouse was the Count de Vaudreuil, a member of the queen's inner circle of courtiers; that the lady they had seen sketching had been none other than the queen herself; and that the man they had seen running had been a messenger hastening to warn the queen that the mob from Paris was marching on Versailles. The curious accent Miss Jourdain had noticed would have been Austrian, as the queen employed many attendants from her native land.

Impressions of the past
The two ladies came up with an explanation of their ghost story. They had not seen ghosts, they said, but had received "impressions." Perhaps the strength of the queen's sense of shock and horror had become imprinted on the Petit Trianon, fixing images in the landscape where she had once been so happy. After the storming of the Palace of Versailles life never returned to normal for the French royal family. Four years later the king and queen met their deaths on the guillotine, and their two surviving children were imprisoned and died in mysterious circumstances.

Temple of Love
Numerous attempts have been made to discredit the ladies' claims. It has been argued, for example, that the elegant Temple de l'Amour *(Temple of Love) was the pavilion where the ladies saw the sinister-looking man on that August afternoon in 1901. When, however, Miss Moberley and Miss Jourdain revisited Versailles, nothing in the modern layout seemed familiar to them. They were resolute in their claim to have seen the garden on their first visit as it was in the 18th century.*

DOUBLE VISION

There are many reports of people appearing in two places at once. More eerie still is the apparition of a doppelganger — a double of yourself that is traditionally regarded as a warning of your impending death.

*I*N 1622, FATHER ALONZO DE BENAVIDES of the Isolita Mission in New Mexico wrote to Pope Urban VIII and King Philip IV of Spain to inquire who had been sent before him to convert the Jumano Indians. Each year when they came to trade, they begged the missionary to send a priest to live among them. They insisted that they had been instructed in Christianity by a "lady in blue." Seeing a painting of a European nun, they said that their lady was similar in appearance, but very young.

This caused some consternation among the Catholic authorities, because, to their certain knowledge, no one had been sent as a missionary to that area. They had, however, heard a report that a 20-year-old nun from Agreda in Spain, Sister Mary of Jesus, claimed to have converted native Indians in North America, without leaving her convent.

Skeptical religious authorities

The church authorities of that time were particularly wary of the claims of religious hysterics, and viewed the case with extreme skepticism. But in this case some investigation was thought to be necessary. It was not until nine years later, however, after

St. Anthony of Padua
This Portuguese saint was reliably reported, by many witnesses, to have appeared at worship in two churches at the same time.

Father Benavides had returned to Spain, that he was sent to interview Sister Mary. By then she was 29 years old and Mother Superior of the convent. Sister Mary could confirm the appearance and customs of the Jumano Indians in accurate detail. She could not explain the phenomenon, but doubted that she had been physically transported to America. She could only suggest that the angels took on her form to work with the natives.

The apparent ability to be in two places at one time (called bilocation)

A missionary of the mind
Sister Mary of Jesus never left
her Spanish convent. But she
claimed to have visited the
Jumano Indians of New Mexico
on more than 50 occasions, and
to have converted them to
Christianity. Her story stood up
under rigorous examination, and
she eventually became a
celebrity and a personal friend
of Philip IV of Spain.

seems to have been a fairly common, and very useful, attribute of various Christian saints and mystics. In 1227 St. Anthony of Padua, the Portuguese Franciscan friar, was apparently the subject of a double sighting in Limoges, in France. On Holy Thursday, he was preaching a sermon in the church of St. Pierre du Queroix at one end of town. He then remembered that he was supposed to be chanting prayers with the friars of his own community in their chapel across town.

A double booking
It is reported that he broke off in the middle of his sermon, knelt down, pulled his hood over his head and remained quite still for several minutes. While this was happening, he is said to have simultaneously appeared in the chapel, chanted the prayers, and then left. As he withdrew from the chapel, he raised his head at the church and continued to address the congregation.

The Indians in New Mexico and the chapel congregation in Limoges may have seen what is known as a "wraith," or "fetch," of the real person. Several explanations have been suggested for these sightings of doubles. Simple hallucination does not appear to account for them, especially when it is reported that more than one person sees

> ## At certain times our astral body is free to move around on its own, and may appear to others as a wraith.

the wraith. Some researchers have suggested that they may in fact be the result of some sort of out-of-the-body or other-body manifestation.

Physical and astral bodies
The idea that different parts of our beings may be able to move separately is an ancient concept. One theory suggests that we are made up of a physical and an astral body. At certain times our astral body is free to move around on its own, and may appear to others as a wraith.

This would explain, for example, another strange and well-documented manifestation of bilocation that occurred on September 22, 1774. St. Alphonsus Liguori, then bishop of St. Agata dei Goti, fell into a deep trance at his episcopal palace near Naples. At the same time he appeared in the chamber of the dying Pope Clement XIV at the Vatican in Rome. He stayed to assist in prayers and consolations and left the chamber after the death of the pontiff. A few minutes later he awoke, back in the palace, and described the scene he had just witnessed.

Twin teachers

One of the best-known cases of bilocation occurred in 1845 at a girls' school near the Baltic Sea in what is now Latvia. The story was told to Robert Dale Owen, an American writer and psychical researcher, by a young German woman, Julie (later Baroness) von Güldenstubbe, who attended the exclusive Pensionat von Neuwelcke.

Emilie Sagée was a young French teacher, popular with both students and staff. But shortly after she arrived at the school, she became the subject of controversy. She was occasionally said to be in more than one place at the same time.

One day her pupils reported that in the middle of a class, while Sagée was working at the blackboard, her double appeared and began to go through the exact same movements but without holding the piece of chalk. In another incident one of the students, Antonie von Wrangle, fainted in fright when she looked in the mirror and,

Bishop Alphonsus Liguori

to her horror, saw Sagée and her double both helping to fix her dress.

The most extraordinary report involved all 42 of the students at the school on a warm summer day in 1846. The girls were in a room with a view of the garden, where Sagée was gathering flowers. When the teacher supervising them went off to speak to the headmistress, Sagée's double appeared at the teacher's chair to watch over the class.

The report continues that the "real" Sagée seemed to be drained of color while the double could be seen. It was as if the double drew its strength from the woman visible in the garden. When questioned, Sagée said that she had felt concerned that the students should not be left unattended. She was then overcome by weariness, just when the double was seen.

A parliamentary appearance

Accounts of bilocation are not restricted to the distant past, and sometimes have the most reliable of witnesses. In 1905 Sir Gilbert Parker, a member of the British Parliament, saw Sir Frederick Carne Rasch sitting in his usual place attending a debate in the House of Commons on a

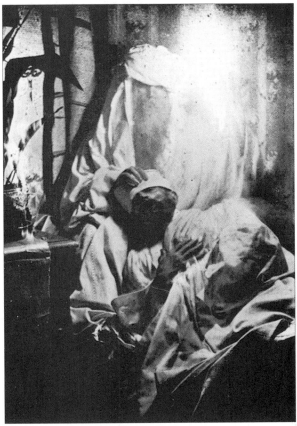

A spirit bodyguard
This memorable photograph, taken at a séance in Paris in 1908, captures the occultist Dr. de Sarak during an out-of-the-body experience. While his physical body remained lying on the couch, it is reported that his astral self visited a friend's apartment. The porter claimed to have seen him arrive, and the doorbell was rung, but there was no one at the door when it was opened. The figure visible behind Dr. de Sarak in this photograph is supposed to be a Grand Master From Beyond, who has the task of guarding his physical body while the astral self is absent.

FAMOUS REFLECTIONS

Many well-known figures have seen wraiths or doppelgangers, not all of which have been forecasts of doom. Such sightings are different from precognitive dreams like that experienced by Abraham Lincoln, foretelling his own assassination; the percipient is awake, and fully aware of his or her surroundings.

Ben Jonson
Not long before the dramatist died in 1637, he saw the wraith of his son. Perhaps this unusual appearance was effected by their strong mutual desire to say farewell before his death.

Doppelgangers in art
Many artists and writers have used the theme of doppelgangers, or personal doubles, in their work. This painting by the pre-Raphaelite Dante Gabriel Rossetti shows two young lovers being confronted by their doppelgangers in a romantic image of impending doom. Oscar Wilde explored the idea of a double in The Portrait of Dorian Gray, *as did the mystery-writer Edgar Allan Poe in his story* William Wilson.

topic of particular interest to him. He found nothing abnormal in this. What was peculiar was that Sir Frederick was stricken with influenza at the time, and according to members of his household, did not leave his bed that day.

Forecast of doom?
Although stories of seeing a double of someone are common enough, in general most people are reluctant to report something that might simply be dismissed as a hallucination. Perhaps such incidents are normally only mentioned or recalled when an unusual event occurs soon afterward. This would account for the popular superstition that seeing your own doppelganger is a forecast of your imminent death or a terrible tragedy.

Guy de Maupassant

The French writer was haunted by a doppelganger toward the end of his life, when he was increasingly plagued by mental illness. On one occasion his double entered the room, sat down opposite him, and dictated exactly what he was writing. Maupassant describes a similar experience in his short story "Lui."

John Donne

One of this 16th-century poet's stock subjects was death and mortality. When in Paris on a visit, his wife appeared to him holding a newborn baby. Sadly, at the very same time back in England, his wife had just given birth to a stillborn child.

Percy Bysshe Shelley

When the 19th-century poet saw his wraith in Italy, it pointed toward the Mediterranean Sea. A short time later he was drowned there while sailing in a small boat. This painting by Louis Fournier depicts the unfortunate poet's cremation on a funeral pyre.

Catherine the Great of Russia

The appearance of her double seated on the imperial throne so incensed the empress that she ordered it to be shot. This had no apparent effect.

JOHANN WOLFGANG VON GOETHE

In his autobiography the German poet Goethe reports two different sightings of doubles. In the first instance, Goethe was riding along the road to Drusenheim, having just said good-bye to his sweetheart, Friederike, when he saw someone who looked exactly like himself riding toward him wearing a gray suit trimmed with gold. These clothes were completely unfamiliar to him.

Eight years later, on another visit to Friederike, he found himself riding in the same direction as the vision, wearing exactly the clothes he had seen eight years before.

Johann Wolfgang von Goethe

A phantom friend

In the second instance, Goethe was on his way home when he came upon his friend Friedrich in the street. Friedrich was wearing Goethe's dressing gown and slippers. When Goethe arrived home, there was his friend dozing by the fire wrapped in the dressing gown and wearing the slippers. Friedrich had borrowed the dressing gown after he had been drenched by a downpour on his way to the poet's home. While he was sleeping, Friedrich dreamed that he had gone off to meet his friend.

Queen Elizabeth I of England

Shortly before her death, the queen saw her doppelganger laid out on her bed, forecasting her demise.

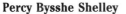

INDEX

Page numbers in **bold** type refer to illustrations and captions.

T

U

V

Veneto, Bartolommeo de, **41**
Venezuela, Sorte Mountain, 58
Vennum, Lurancy, 114–115, **115**
Versailles, 132–135, **133**, **135**
Victorio (Apache chief), 90
Victorio Peak, 90–91
Vikings, **42**
    burial mound, **48**, **74**

W

Y

PHOTOGRAPHIC SOURCES ──